# CAUSES

# O IN E PE

MARTYN RADY

# CAUSES AND CONSEQUENCES

The Arab-Israeli Conflict
The End of Apartheid
The Collapse of Communism in Eastern Europe
The Rise of Japan and the Pacific Rim
The Second World War
The Vietnam War

Published by Evans Brothers Limited
2A Portman Mansions
Chiltern Street
London W1M 1LE
England

First published in 1995

ISBN 0 237 51381 1

Planning and production by The Creative Publishing Company
Edited by Christine Lawrie
Designed by Ian Winton

# CONTENTS

# INTRODUCTION

**E**ast Berlin: 6 October 1989 — the fortieth anniversary of the founding of the East German state. All the communist leaders of Eastern Europe were gathered together in the East German capital to take part in the event. The principal guest was the leader of the Soviet Union, Mikhail Gorbachev. The anniversary was marked with speeches of praise for East Germany, with each of the communist leaders embracing one another, and in the evening with a vast torchlight procession through the centre of the capital.

Despite the celebrations, communism in both East Germany and Eastern Europe was in deep crisis. Already in Hungary and Poland, the communists had given up their hold on power and both countries were on the brink of becoming democracies. In East

*The Soviet leader, Mikhail Gorbachev, greets the communist leader of East Germany, Erich Honecker, in October, 1989. Within the month, Honecker would be overthrown.*

Germany, the days preceding the anniversary had been marked by fierce street protests against the communist government. Even as the torchlight procession made its way through East Berlin, police with riot-shields and dogs were breaking up demonstrations in other parts of the city.

Behind the scenes, the friendship shown in public by the communist chiefs was replaced by criticism and argument. Gorbachev told the East German leader, Erich Honecker, that he could not hope to survive the crisis in his country unless he introduced far-reaching reforms. 'Those who delay are punished by life itself,' advised the Soviet leader. But Honecker stubbornly replied, 'Those who are declared dead usually live a long time.'

Gorbachev was right. In less than a fortnight, Honecker had been forced to resign. The next month, communism in East Germany collapsed entirely. Demonstrations and protests swiftly brought down the communist governments in Czechoslovakia, Bulgaria and Romania. Two years later, it was the turn of the Soviet Union. In 1991, the Communist Party was outlawed and by the end of the year, the Soviet Union had itself ceased to exist.

Communism had lasted in Eastern Europe for more than forty years. Yet its collapse was assured within the space of just a few months in 1989. This book will examine what communism meant for East Europeans and why it was in the end so rapidly overthrown. It will also consider what happened in Eastern Europe after 1989. Although the countries of Eastern Europe are now democracies, they face many social, political and economic problems. As the example of the former Yugoslavia suggests, the scale of these difficulties may be sufficient to lead to tragedy and bloodshed.

*The Berlin Wall, symbol of the Cold War division of Europe, falls in November 1989.*

Many thousands of citizens had formed a dense row for their arrival. From the midst rang out cheers for Erich Honecker and Mikhail Gorbachev. . . . The two leading personalities were greeted everywhere with great applause.

An East German news agency report on the meeting of Mikhail Gorbachev and Erich Honecker on 6 October 1989.

# THE COMMUNIST TAKE-OVER

## EASTERN EUROPE BEFORE COMMUNISM

*Between the two World Wars, the economies of the Eastern European countries remained backward, based primarily on agriculture. Typically, the harvest was gathered by hand, without the help of modern farm machinery.*

From the late middle ages until the beginning of the twentieth century, most of the peoples of Eastern Europe lived under foreign rule. By the late nineteenth century, the whole region had been divided up between four great empires: the Turkish (also called the Ottoman), Russian, German and Habsburg (also called the Austro-Hungarian).

During the nineteenth century, the peoples of Eastern Europe became greatly affected by nationalism. Nationalism is the belief that a nation or people

deserves to have its own independent state and should not be forced to live under foreign domination.

The spread of nationalist beliefs in Eastern Europe resulted in a series of rebellions against foreign rule. During the course of the nineteenth century, Turkey was forced to grant independence to Greece, Romania, Bulgaria and Serbia. The First World War dealt a death-blow to the remaining empires of Eastern Europe. None had the resources to endure a long conflict. In 1917 the Russian Empire collapsed under the strain of the war. The next year, the German and Habsburg Empires disintegrated.

In 1919 statesmen from Europe and the United States met at the Paris Peace Conference to draw up a new map of Eastern Europe. They were convinced that new nation states should be set up to take the place of the old empires. An independent Polish state was, therefore, created out of the ruins of the German, Habsburg and Russian Empires. Austria and Hungary were made into independent states.

In a few places, new states were created by merging together peoples who at the time were thought to be closely related. In 1919, the Czechs and Slovaks were joined together in a state called Czechoslovakia. In much the same way, Serbs, Croats, Slovenes, Bosnians and Macedonians were united in the state of Yugoslavia which was originally called the Kingdom of Serbs, Croats and Slovenes.

Between the First and Second World Wars, Eastern Europe consisted of small, independent states most of which were entirely new political creations. Few of these states, however, prospered. Most remained economically backward and their populations comprised mainly poor peasant farmers. Although attempts were made to establish democratic governments, the trend in much of the region was towards dictatorship and military rule. Only Czechoslovakia remained a democracy.

In 1933 Adolf Hitler came to power in Germany and he made no secret of his aim

*Nazi Germany, led by Adolf Hitler, began to expand aggressively into Eastern Europe in the late 1930s. The German attack on Poland in September 1939 led to the Second World War.*

that Germany should dominate the lands and peoples of Eastern Europe. In 1938, Hitler occupied Austria. The next year, he took over the western half of Czechoslovakia and then attacked Poland. Hitler's aggressive actions in Eastern Europe forced Britain and France to declare war on Germany in 1939 and were the direct cause of the Second World War.

## COMMUNISM AND THE SOVIET UNION

The Soviet Union had been established after the collapse of the Russian Empire in 1917 and was a communist state. Communism is a series of beliefs originally put forward by the German philosopher, Karl Marx (1818-83). Marx's theories were revised and made more practical by Vladimir Illyich Lenin (1870-1924), who became the first leader of the Soviet Union.

*This map shows the divisions of Central and Eastern Europe at the beginning of the nineteenth century. The forces of nationalism were already weakening the bonds of empire, a process that would be completed by the First World War.*

According to communists, the fairest type of society can only be achieved by the state taking control of nearly every aspect of human life. Communists argue that the working class has throughout its history been cheated and exploited by factory owners and landowners. A communist government, so it is claimed, would arrange affairs differently. By taking control of business and industry, it would be able to act in the interests of the workers.

Joseph Stalin, who ruled the Soviet Union from 1928 to 1953, believed that a communist state, in order to achieve its goals, needed to eliminate all private enterprise and to concentrate on building up its economic power. During the 1930s, massive state-owned industrial complexes were established throughout the Soviet Union. The peasants were forced to give up their private plots of land and to work together on state-run farms or collectives.

*The borders within Central and Eastern Europe were dramatically changed by the Paris Peace Conference of 1919, when new nation states were set up to take the place of the old empires. These new borders remained unchanged until the Second World War.*

*During the 1930s, the peasantry of the Soviet Union were forced to give up their private plots of land and to work instead on state farms, or collectives. Conditions were generally very poor. There was often a lack of modern transport and even camels were used to pull wagons. Nevertheless, as in this picture, the peasants were expected to show their support for the new collectives.*

No comrades, the pace must not be slackened. On the contrary we must quicken it. . . .
    To slow down the tempo [of industrialization] means to lag behind. And those who lag behind are beaten. The history of Old Russia shows that, because of her backwardness, she was constantly being defeated. Beaten because of her backwardness — military, cultural, political, industrial and agricultural backwardness. . . . We are fifty or a hundred years behind the advanced countries. We must make good this lag in ten years. Either we do it or they crush us.

The text of this speech by Stalin to senior members of the Communist Party in 1931, reveals his fear that the Soviet Union stands in danger of attack.

Although Stalin partially succeeded in making the Soviet Union a modern, industrial power, he did so at tremendous human cost. At least ten million people died in famines caused by his agricultural policies; an even greater number perished as political prisoners in labour-camps. Most communists today believe that Stalin betrayed communism by embarking upon policies which were too ruthless and inhumane.

As a convinced communist, Stalin believed that he had an obligation to spread communism abroad. He also feared that the Soviet Union was in danger of being attacked by the non-communist or 'capitalist' European powers. In order to protect itself from invasion, he believed the Soviet Union urgently needed to expand its territory and influence. Following the outbreak of the Second World War, Stalin occupied eastern Poland and the Baltic states of Lithuania, Latvia and Estonia.

In August 1939, Stalin had negotiated a non-aggression pact with Hitler. By doing so, Stalin hoped to keep the Soviet Union out of the Second World War. In 1941, however, Hitler unexpectedly attacked the Soviet Union, rapidly driving Stalin's army into retreat. Within a few months, German troops were on the outskirts of the Soviet Union's two most important cities, Moscow and Leningrad. Only the onset of winter prevented the Germans from achieving an absolute victory over the Soviet Union.

Over the next four years, Stalin's armies, now on the side of the Allies, fought a desperate war against the Germans. By 1944, Soviet troops had pushed the Germans out of the territory of the Soviet Union. The next year, the Soviet armies pursued the Germans across Eastern Europe. Eventually in April 1945 they reached the German capital, Berlin. Their part in the victory over Nazi Germany was, however, achieved at the cost of 40 million Soviet lives.

## COMMUNISM AND EASTERN EUROPE

The experience of the Second World War confirmed Stalin's belief that the Soviet Union would never be safe unless it was protected by a belt of territories in Eastern Europe. Stalin was sure that the western powers, and in particular the United States, having defeated Germany, now wanted to overthrow communist power in the Soviet Union. Stalin was also convinced that communism represented the best way of life for the peoples of Eastern Europe and that it was his duty, as a communist, to spread communism there.

At the meeting with the leaders of the United States and Great Britain, held in Yalta in the Crimea in February 1945, Stalin agreed that there would be free elections in the countries of Eastern Europe occupied by his armies. Instead, however, he took the opportunity to seize full political control of the region by force. Soviet troops and secret police arrested non-communist politicians and gradually took over the governments in each of the East European states. Rigged elections were then held which resulted in communist victories. Once in power, the Communist Parties passed laws making all the other political parties illegal.

Between 1945 and 1948, Poland, Romania, Hungary, Czechoslovakia, Bulgaria, Albania and Yugoslavia all became communist states. In the eastern part of Germany, which was under Soviet occupation, a communist government was installed and, in 1949, a separate East German state was set up. The capital city of East Germany, Berlin, remained divided between a communist eastern half and a western half which was

*April, 1945: Soviet troops hoist the Hammer and Sickle, the flag of the Soviet Union, on the top of the parliament building in Berlin.*

*After the Second World War most countries of Eastern Europe were under Soviet control. The common border between these countries and the rest of Europe was known as the Iron Curtain. Albania was more influenced by Chinese than Russian communism and was politically isolated from both Eastern and Western Europe. This map shows the borders in the area from 1946 to 1989. The heavy black line represents the Iron Curtain border.*

The electoral law gave every advantage to the communists. Polls were set up in factories and barracks where [their] agents could bring direct pressure on workers and soldiers. Electoral lists were hastily compiled so that no real check could be made on inaccuracies. . . . On 19 November 1946, the Romanian people went to the polls in an election in which every fraudulent, violent and unscrupulous device ever used in the Balkans was brought into full play.

From R.L. Wolff, *The Balkans in Our Time* (Harvard University Press, 1956).

occupied by troops from Britain, France and America.

The communist governments of Eastern Europe rapidly converted their states into 'satellites' of the Soviet Union. The communist leaders barely followed policies of their own, acting instead only on Stalin's orders. They copied Stalin's industrial and agricultural policies by building massive new factories and forcing the peasantry into collectives. In 1949 the communist states of Eastern Europe were joined together in an economic union known as the Council for Mutual Economic Assistance (or Comecon).

Soviet influence was, however, weak in Yugoslavia. Although a communist country, no Soviet forces were stationed in Yugoslavia. Stalin's attempt to impose his own military and economic policies on Yugoslavia was resented by the Yugoslav communist leader, Marshal Tito. In 1948, Tito broke with the Soviet Union. Although Yugoslavia remained a communist state, it now began to pursue an independent and neutral policy.

# THE ECONOMIC SITUATION

## THE INHERITANCE

Eastern Europe had been ruined economically by the Second World War. The passage of the German and Soviet armies had devastated a large part of the region. By 1945, many of the principal cities and industrial centres had been reduced to rubble. At the end of the war, industrial production in Eastern Europe had fallen to below a half of what it had been in 1939.

In addition, the war had claimed many lives. The Soviet Union is thought to have lost over 40 million of its citizens. Poland had 6 million dead and Yugoslavia 1.7 million. The educated and professional classes suffered particularly heavy losses. By 1945, the Polish middle class had been reduced by a third while Hungary had lost virtually all of its educated Jewish population in the Nazi concentration camps.

After the war, a large part of the German population of Eastern Europe was expelled — 3 million were forced out of Czechoslovakia and 8 million from Poland. The Germans of Eastern Europe had lived in the region for many centuries. Nevertheless, they were considered in 1945 to be partly guilty of starting the war. Many of

*The defeat of Nazi Germany was achieved at tremendous cost. As this February 1945 photograph of the Hungarian capital, Budapest, shows, many of the major East European cities were devastated in the fighting.*

those expelled had been skilled craftsmen, engineers and factory owners.

The communists therefore took over a region which had not only been devastated by the Second World War but which had also lost a large part of the population upon whose experience economic recovery depended.

## THE COLD WAR

Western Europe and the United States feared that the Soviet Union wanted to expand even further into Europe. For its part, the Soviet Union believed that the United States was so opposed to communism as to be ready to go to war. The distrust between the West and the Soviet Union led to the period known as the Cold War, which lasted from the end of the Second World War to the 1980s. During the Cold War, the countries of Eastern Europe were joined together in a military alliance led by the Soviet Union, which was known as the Warsaw Pact. The Warsaw Pact was opposed by a military alliance of western countries known as the North Atlantic Treaty Organization (NATO).

As a result of the Cold War, Eastern Europe was denied access to the loans and financial support which the United States made available to Western Europe. It had instead to rely upon its own diminished industrial resources. On top of this, military competition between NATO and the Warsaw Pact forced the communist governments of Eastern Europe to spend money that they could ill afford on arms and weapons. To begin with, the Soviet Union and its allies managed to keep pace militarily with the West. In 1949 the Soviet Union exploded an atom bomb and, eight years later, launched the first earth satellite or 'sputnik'. In 1961, the Russian Yuri Gagarin became the first man in space.

By the 1970s, however, the cost of the Cold War was beginning severely to undermine the economies of the East European communist countries. As a result, the Soviet Union responded positively to attempts led by West Germany to relax the tension between East and West. The process of easing relations, or of *détente*, led to Eastern Europe receiving some limited economic assistance from Western Europe and the United States. Nevertheless, restrictions still remained on what help might be given to Eastern Europe. In particular, the export of hi-tech and computer goods from West to East was forbidden while the communists were still in power.

The people themselves . . . lack animation. Even the children seemingly well cared-for, are unnaturally subdued, at any rate in public. Almost the entire nation, soldiers and sportsmen apart, gives the appearance of physical and mental dejection. . . . Food is expensive although of indifferent quality, and meat, bread and eggs are frequently scarce. . . . Shoddy consumer goods are displayed with more art than prodigality in shop windows. Prices are extortionately high; wages low. Living accommodation is grossly overcrowded; public transport is antiquated and inefficient. Highways are poor, while most of the byways outside the capital are no better than rutted tracks. Schools and hospitals are drab and ill-equipped.

A British diplomat describes Hungary in January 1956.

# INDUSTRY, AGRICULTURE AND THE ENVIRONMENT

The Second World War and the Cold War explain some of the difficulties faced by the East European economies in the post-war era. Nevertheless, substantial blame must also attach to the communists themselves for the region's poor economic performance.

The East European communist leaders followed Stalin in believing that the most efficient economies were those which depended on heavy industry, collectivized agriculture and state planning. Accordingly in the 1940s and 1950s much stress was put on the construction of new factories and industrial plants. At the same time, labourers in the countryside were forced to join collective farms and to give up cultivating their own private lands. Profits in both industry and agriculture were ploughed back into the economy and only a little was paid in wages.

In the early years, communist economics seemed to work. Production levels increased dramatically, growing at a rate of over 10 per cent a year. By the late 1950s, however, the economies of the East European countries were beginning to show signs of strain. The factories had been constructed too hastily and with out-of-date technology (one steel plant in Hungary, built in 1949 and working right up until the 1980s, was based on American designs dating from the 1920s). The quality of goods which they manufactured was usually poor, and many electrical appliances were unsafe to use.

*The rapid growth of industry in post-war Eastern Europe was achieved at the cost of massive environmental damage to large parts of the region as this picture of Upper Silesia, in Poland, shows.*

Collectivized agriculture was also very inefficient and never received sufficient money to help it
improve. In large parts of Eastern Europe, the ox-
plough was still the norm and the harvest was gathered
by scythe. In the summer, it was common for schoolchildren to be made to work unpaid in the countryside.

The planning system used in Eastern Europe only
made matters worse. Every item of production, from nuts
and bolts to industrial turbines, depended on an arrangement whereby government ministers, Communist Party
officials and factory managers would draw up a compre-
hensive plan establishing priorities and targets. This system produced mountains of paper (the Romanian plan
was a hundred metres long in its final, abbreviated draft!)
but scarcely made for efficient management. The
rationing of even basic goods continued in some parts of
Eastern Europe right up until the 1980s. The waiting list
for a new car was usually about ten years.

Although the communists prided themselves on
having no unemployment in their countries, a large part
of the workforce remained under-occupied at work. The
low level of wages was a disincentive to effort and led to
the saying: 'They pretend to pay us and we pretend to
work.' More seriously, it resulted in the frequent theft of
tools and furnishings from the workplace.

Communist industrial policy earned the description 'lunar economics' on account of the way it scarred
and damaged the landscape of Eastern Europe. New
industries were built with little thought for the environ-
ment. In northern Czechoslovakia and the southern parts
of Poland and East Germany, the construction of steel
plants and generating stations resulted in such high sul-
phur-dioxide emissions as to precipitate acid rain which
destroyed the local forests. In Romania, the carbon factory at Copsa Mica deposited a thick layer of black soot
over wide areas of the countryside. Pollution was so bad
there that it actually snowed black flakes.

There is no unem-
ployment, but
nobody works.
Nobody works, but
the plan is fulfilled.
The plan is fulfilled,
but there is nothing
to buy.
There is nothing to
buy, but you can find
anything.
You can find any-
thing, but everybody
steals.
Everybody steals,
but nothing has been
stolen.
Nothing has been
stolen, but it's
impossible to work.
It's impossible to
work, but there's no
unemployment.

*The Eight Wonders of
the Communist
Economy* Anonymous

## DEBT

Until the early 1960s, it was still possible to believe that
the communist economic system might eventually suc-
ceed and that the East European economies could in time
overtake those of Western Europe. Eastern Europe, however, failed to benefit from the international boom of the
1960s and was particularly badly affected by the global
recession of the 1970s.

As the weakness of the East European economies became ever more obvious, the communist leaders started to borrow large sums of money from Western Europe and the United States. They then invested the borrowed money in industry in the hope of speeding a recovery. Frequently, however, they backed the wrong industries — unprofitable steel mills and coal mines — and then found themselves unable to repay the money that they had borrowed.

During the 1980s, the communist leaders of Eastern Europe realized the painful truth that their policies were just not working. Not only were their countries lagging behind Western Europe but also their economies were so technologically backward that they had no share in the new computer-revolution sweeping the rest of the developed world. On top of this, from the late 1970s onwards, the United States began rearming. Presidents Carter (1977-81) and Reagan (1981-89) announced plans for the deployment of new nuclear missiles in Western Europe, for a bomber-aircraft which could not be picked up on radar, and for a space system which would eliminate nuclear weapons while they were still in flight.

The communist leaders in the Soviet Union and Eastern Europe were eager to match the United States in military power and nuclear technology. They realized, however, that their countries lacked both the technical and financial resources to achieve this goal.

*In 1983, American President Reagan launched his Strategic Defence Initiative (SDI). Although it got no further than the planning stage, this diagram shows how it was expected to work. A nuclear missile launched by an aggressor nation (1) is detected by a satellite (2), which feeds data to a ground-based laser (3). A laser beam is directed at a mirror satellite (4), which reflects the beam to a battle satellite (5). The beam is directed at the missile, destroying it. SDI, and other elaborate Western military technology was beyond the means of the communist governments of Eastern Europe.*

# COMMUNIST SOCIETY

## STATE TERROR

It was at the beginning of the fifties, that the atmosphere of real physical violence was created. Concentration camps existed for interning people, for the so-called class enemies, simply because they belonged to a different social layer, including for instance, richer farmers and landowners, members of the middle class. The period didn't last long, it's true, but its implications can be felt today. It created an atmosphere of fear and anticipation of more repression and violence against those who did not conform.

The memories of a former Czech dissident.

Nowhere in Eastern Europe had communist governments been established by the will of the people in free and democratic elections. The communists had not been voted into power but had, instead, seized it by force in the wake of the defeat of Nazism. In addition, the communists claimed that their way of running an economy would guarantee a high level of industrial efficiency and production which would ensure increased material benefits for the people. When these claims were exposed as largely unattainable, the population became even more resentful of communism.

Widespread dislike of communist rule meant that the governments of Eastern Europe had to rely heavily upon the secret police to suppress dissent. The communist secret police employed networks of informers, both in the workplace and in society at large, to keep track of possible opponents and they regularly opened private mail and tapped telephones. In the 1940s and 50s, hundreds of thousands of East Europeans, who were suspected of being anti-communist, were arrested. Their trials were usually conducted unfairly with a hired crowd in the courtroom calling for a verdict of guilty. The evidence produced by the prosecution was frequently invented. Often, while awaiting trial, the defendants were tortured to make them sign false confessions.

In most of the communist countries of Eastern Europe, permission to travel abroad to a non-communist country was only rarely given. The communist governments feared that people once allowed to leave would never return. On their borders with the non-communist countries, the police set up barbed-wire barriers to prevent people escaping abroad. In 1961 a fortified line was built through the middle of Berlin to prevent East Germans escaping to the non-communist part of the city.

*The Berlin Wall was built in 1961 to prevent East German citizens escaping to the West. Construction of the Wall often divided friends and families. Here, a West Berlin girl and her boyfriend talk over the Wall to her mother in East Berlin.*

## GOULASH COMMUNISM

During the late 1960s, most of the communist governments of Eastern Europe relaxed their use of state terror (the main exceptions were Albania and Romania). Instead of attempting to keep their populations under control by use of the police, the communists tried to buy the people's co-operation by increasing the production of consumer goods. This technique was first applied in Hungary as a result of which it was known as 'goulash communism'. (Goulash is a popular meat dish in Hungary.)

Under goulash communism an increasing supply and variety of goods were made available in the shops. East Europeans now had access to, for instance, different styles of clothing and shoes whereas previously the choice had been restricted to only one or two designs. Year by year, new items found their way on to storeshelves. In 1979, salami could be bought for the first time in many years in Hungarian supermarkets; the next year scented soap. A limited supply of western goods, such as music cassettes and quality electrical goods, was also imported into Eastern Europe, although these items were always sold at high prices.

In the workplace, the communists tried to win the support of the population by increasing wages. Through the state-run trade unions, workers and their families were offered cheap holiday trips to other parts of Eastern Europe.

*As part of their attempt to buy the support and goodwill of the population, the communist governments of Eastern Europe provided plentiful, cheap holidays. This is the Black Sea resort of Yalta in 1974.*

Treason, treason
Cunning, cold, calculating . . .
Broken promises, broken light,
White is black and black is white . . .
Don't talk back, turn the other cheek . . .
Talk out of line if you dare.
Don't make me look, I don't want to see.
Is everyone a traitor or is it just me?
Treason sneeks into your bed.

Lyrics of a Polish rock song from 1983.

# HEALTH, HOUSING AND EDUCATION

During the period of goulash communism the communist governments of Eastern Europe increased the supply of medicine and homes for the population. Whereas before families had often been crammed together in single rooms, from the 1960s onwards a massive rebuilding programme was undertaken. The cities of Eastern Europe became surrounded by estates of high-rise blocks. Nevertheless, the housing supply remained insufficient and waiting lists were long. In the 1980s it was still usual for most newly-married couples to live with their parents, often in crowded two- or three-room apartments. Although some homes were available for private purchase, their cost was normally too high for most people.

Throughout Eastern Europe, the communists introduced a system of free health care. In some countries, most notably Hungary, the medical service was of a standard equivalent to that in Western Europe. Hungarian doctors pioneered new treatments for disabled children, which have since been copied in the West. Nevertheless, in most of the region the proper drugs were often in short supply. In Romania, many hospital patients were forced to share beds.

Like health care, education in the communist

countries was free. At the age of 14 or 15, most children went to work. A minority progressed either to technical schools for vocational training or to grammar schools as a preparation for university and the professions. One of the greatest achievements of the communist period was the virtual elimination of illiteracy in Eastern Europe and the creation of an educated and trained workforce.

## INNER EMIGRATION

The majority of the population of Eastern Europe responded to communist rule by what was known as 'inner emigration'. Unable to change the system of government, they retreated into their own private worlds and tried to avoid having anything to do with politics. Family life at home, the building of summer houses in the countryside, and the cultivation of small allotments became the main interests of many East Europeans.

*Although medical treatment was provided free in most East European countries, conditions in the hospitals, like this children's hospital in Romania, were often primitive and crowded.*

The frustration which many of these people felt gave inner emigration a more unpleasant side. During the period of communist rule, alcoholism and alcohol-related illnesses became widespread. In Hungary between 1948 and 1984 the suicide rate doubled, making it one of the highest in Europe.

Among young people, discontent with communism most commonly expressed itself in fashion and music. East European teenagers eagerly searched out the latest western designs and pop songs and they made a cult of everything American. The East German government was so alarmed by this trend that for a short time it even tried to ban blue jeans. Rock music was another means by which teenagers were able show their dissatisfaction with communism. The lyrics of rock songs frequently contained lines which were highly critical of the communist governments in power.

23

# REVOLTS OF THE REPRESSED

## PROTESTS IN THE 1950s

R esistance to communist rule often, however, took a more violent form than inner emigration. One of the earliest protests happened in 1953. In East Berlin and other East German cities, workers demonstrated against the communist government's attempts to increase the length of the working day. When the government refused to give way, the workers called a general strike. Only the intervention of the Soviet army and the deaths of several hundred protesting workers prevented the collapse of communist rule in East Germany.

*Workers and students gather in the streets of East Berlin during the East German Rising of 1953.*

*Soviet tanks on the streets of Budapest during the Hungarian Revolution of 1956. Only massive Soviet intervention prevented the collapse of Hungary's communist government.*

The rebellion in East Germany occurred in the same year as the death of the Soviet leader, Stalin. Throughout his long period in office, Stalin had maintained a tight grip both on the Soviet Union and, after 1945, on the satellite-states of Eastern Europe. Stalin was succeeded as Soviet leader by Nikita Khrushchev. Once in power, Khrushchev announced that he would not follow the same harsh policies as his predecessor.

Khrushchev's rise to power seemed to signal a new era when communist rule would not be enforced as violently as it had been under Stalin. In response, students and young people in Hungary demonstrated in October 1956 against the continued rule in their country of communist hardliners previously appointed by Stalin. With the approval of the Soviet Union, a moderate communist, Imre Nagy, took over the government. Nevertheless, demands for change continued to grow. Under the pressure of street demonstrations, Nagy announced that he would hold democratic elections and that Hungary would leave the Warsaw Pact and become a neutral state.

This was too much for Khrushchev. In early November, the Soviet army invaded Hungary and tanks moved into the centre of the Hungarian capital, Budapest. The Hungarians resisted the invasion heroically, but were nevertheless rapidly defeated. Around 20,000 participants in the 'Hungarian Revolution' were arrested, of whom at least 2,000 were executed. Imre Nagy was hanged.

## THE 'PRAGUE SPRING'

Twelve years later, Soviet tanks had to invade yet another East European country. In 1968 Alexander Dubcek was appointed the communist leader of Czechoslovakia. He promised 'socialism with a human face', by which he meant a kinder and more tolerant type of communism. He relaxed state censorship of the newspapers and media, and allowed political issues to be discussed more openly. The reforms introduced by Dubcek gave hope to many Czechs and Slovaks who called the period of his rule the 'Prague Spring'.

*In 1968, the Czechoslovak leader, Alexander Dubcek, tried to introduce a more tolerant type of communism. Within a few months, the Soviet Union and its Warsaw Pact allies invaded Czechoslovakia and put an end to Dubcek's experiment.*

The Soviet Union, however, viewed the changes in Czechoslovakia with concern. The Soviet leaders feared that the Communist Party might lose control in Czechoslovakia. Having failed to convince Dubcek that he should change his policies, the Soviet Union with its Warsaw Pact allies invaded Czechoslovakia in August 1968. The invasion of Czechoslovakia was subsequently justified by the Soviet leader, Leonid Brezhnev. Brezhnev claimed that it was the right of communist states to intervene in another communist state if communism was threatened there.

*In Prague, the Czechoslovak capital, the Soviet-led invasion of 1968 was met with demonstrations and protests, led mainly by students and young people.*

The resistance in Czechoslovakia to the Soviet intervention was less bloody than in Hungary in 1956. Most Czechs and Slovaks responded peacefully, arguing with, rather than attacking, the invading troops. Nevertheless, several dozen people were killed in the course of demonstrations.

Following the Soviet invasion, Dubcek was removed from office. Over the next few years, a hard-line communist government began the process of what became known as 'normalization': returning Czechoslovakia to what had been 'normal' before 1968. Many thousands of Czechs and Slovaks lost their jobs and suffered persecution for having been supporters of Dubcek's reforms.

## CHARTER 77

Charter 77 is a free, informal, open community of peoples of different convictions, different faiths and different professions united by the will to strive, individually and collectively, for the respect of civic and human rights in our own country and throughout the world. . . .

Charter 77 springs from a background of friendship and solidarity among people who share our concern for those ideals that have inspired, and continue to inspire, their lives and their work. . . .

*The Manifesto of Charter 77*

Opposition to communist rule continued in Czechoslovakia despite normalization. Strong criticism of the government was expressed in secretly produced books and pamphlets. In December 1976 some of the leading anti-communists or 'dissidents' in Czechoslovakia founded a group known as 'Charter 77' (the movement's declaration was dated 1 January 1977). It was the aim of Charter 77 to draw attention to the communist government's treatment of political opponents.

One of the founding members of Charter 77 was the playwright, Vaclav Havel, who later became the first president of Czechoslovakia following the collapse of communism in 1989. Members of Charter 77 faced arrest and imprisonment at the hands of the secret police. Nevertheless, their example gave hope to many Czechs and Slovaks and inspired others to found opposition groups.

## POLISH SOLIDARITY

Citizens of the Polish People's Republic!

I address you today as a soldier and the head of government in Poland. I address you on a matter of paramount importance.

Our country stands at the edge of an abyss. . . .

I hereby announce that today a Military Council of National Salvation has been constituted.

In conformity with the provisions of the constitution, at midnight tonight the Council of State proclaimed martial law throughout the whole country.

General Jaruzelski declaring martial law, 13 December 1981.

In Czechoslovakia, the opposition to communist rule was led in the main by intellectuals — playwrights, artists, journalists and actors. In Poland, however, the struggle was led primarily by trade union workers.

Throughout the 1950s, 60s and 70s, there had been outbreaks of unrest in Poland. In 1980, price rises made necessary by the poor condition of the economy, set off strikes throughout the country. In the port of Gdansk, the strikes were led by an electrician called Lech Walesa. The strikes forced the government to give way to the demand made by the workers that they be allowed their own trade union. By the end of the year, Solidarity, the trade union led by Walesa, had 10 million members.

During 1981 the influence and reputation of Solidarity and of its counterpart in the countryside, Rural Solidarity, grew. Many members of the Communist Party joined the new trade unions. By the end of the year it was clear that communist rule in Poland was near collapse. In order to prevent the Soviet Union invading the country to restore communist control, the Polish premier, General Jaruzelski, led a military revolt or *coup d'état*. The leading communists

were all replaced by army generals and Walesa and the other trade-unionists were briefly imprisoned. The Solidarity trade union was declared illegal.

By his action Jaruzelski probably saved Poland from a Soviet invasion. However, the *coup* of 1981 left the Polish Communist Party demoralized and the Polish people sullen and resentful. Nor did the banning of Solidarity prevent further waves of strikes and industrial unrest.

None of the rebellions and movements discussed in this chapter — the revolt in East Germany in 1953, the Hungarian Revolution of 1956, the Prague Spring of 1968, Charter 77 and Polish Solidarity — was able to bring about the collapse of communist rule in Eastern Europe. Direct Soviet intervention or, as in 1981, the risk of intervention, prevented the overthrow of communism.

With each new outbreak of discontent, however, the failure of the Communist Parties of Eastern Europe to deliver on their promise of a better life became more obvious. By the 1980s it was clear that all the East European Communist Parties could rely upon for survival was a policy of repression and the continued military support of the Soviet Union.

*The leader of the Polish Solidarity trade union, Lech Walesa, is carried aloft by his supporters through the streets of the Polish capital, Warsaw, in November 1981. Less than a month after this photograph was taken, Walesa was arrested, Solidarity was banned and martial law was declared in Poland.*

# THE GORBACHEV PHENOMENON

## THE RISE OF MIKHAIL GORBACHEV

*Mikhail Gorbachev's reforms were enthusiastically supported by many East Europeans. In this July 1988 photograph of a visit to the Polish city of Szczecin, Gorbachev is being applauded by its citizens. Behind him, in the dark glasses, stands the Polish communist leader, General Jaruzelski.*

Nikita Khrushchev, Leonid Brezhnev, Yuri Andropov and Konstantin Chernenko, who in turn ruled the Soviet Union from 1953 to 1985, followed less brutal policies than Joseph Stalin.

Nevertheless, each was a committed communist and each was equally determined to maintain the Soviet domination of Eastern Europe.

To begin with, Mikhail Gorbachev, who became Soviet leader in 1985, seemed little different from his predecessors. Although the economy of the Soviet Union was in deep crisis, Gorbachev thought it could be rescued simply by eliminating the endemic corruption and making the population work harder. His first slogan was therefore not the word *perestroika* ('rebuilding') with which he is usually associated, but *uskorenie* ('acceleration').

## GORBACHEV'S REFORMS

Towards the end of 1986, however, Gorbachev's policies began to change. Instead of tinkering with the communist economic system, Gorbachev launched a full-scale reform programme. By then, Gorbachev had realized that the economy of the Soviet Union could only be saved by a process of *perestroika* and by reorganizing it entirely. Acceleration was not enough.

In keeping with the new slogan, attempts were made to restructure Soviet industry by giving managers more freedom to make decisions. The old method of centralized state-planning was largely abandoned. Small private businesses were also allowed for the first time in the Soviet Union since the 1920s.

Gorbachev's reforms affected not just the economy but politics as well. Under the slogan of *glasnost* or 'openness', Gorbachev encouraged criticism of Soviet policies and he welcomed suggestions for change. Censorship was almost entirely abolished; books banned under Gorbachev's predecessors were now sold quite openly; and most political prisoners were freed.

These reforms were opposed by a large section of the Soviet Communist Party which feared that Gorbachev's policies would lead in the end to the abandonment of communism. In order to reduce their influence, Gorbachev increasingly pressed for *demokratizatsiya* or 'democratization'. By democratization Gorbachev meant elections which would have the consequence of replacing the old communists with his own supporters. Elections to the Soviet parliament, or Congress of People's Deputies, held in the spring of

The fact that European states belong to different social systems is a reality. . . . Social and political orders in one or another country have changed in the past and may change in the future. However, this is exclusively the affair of the peoples themselves; it is their choice. Any interference in internal affairs and any attempts to restrict the sovereignty of states — either friends and allies or anyone else — are inadmissable.

Mikhail Gorbachev explains that the Soviet Union will no longer interfere in the internal affairs of the countries of Eastern Europe, 6 July 1989.

*One of Gorbachev's first acts as Soviet leader was to release the dissident scientist, Andrei Sakharov, from exile. In 1989, Sakharov was elected a member of the Soviet parliament, the Congress of People's Deputies.*

1989 resulted, as Gorbachev intended, in substantial gains for his followers.

## GORBACHEV AND EASTERN EUROPE

Rebuilding, openness and democratization: each of these was a major threat to the communist governments in Eastern Europe. The economies of the East European satellites stood as urgently in need of reform as that of the Soviet Union. Yet few East European communist leaders were ready to take on the challenge of *perestroika* in their own countries. Openness, likewise, promised to undermine political systems that had long been built on repression and censorship; and democratization, if attempted in Eastern Europe, would surely mean the rapid replacement of the old-style communists presently in power.

All across Eastern Europe opposition groups began to press their own governments to adopt the new policies followed in the Soviet Union. Demands for reform began to be made even within the East European Communist Parties. On his visits to East European cities, Gorbachev was regularly greeted by large applauding crowds calling his name. The excitement which his reforms aroused in Eastern Europe prompted a joke on the streets of the Czechoslovak capital, Prague: 'A Soviet invasion is planned. The Czechoslovak communists are going to invade the Soviet Union in order to defend communism.'

Throughout his period as Soviet leader, Gorbachev had been re-examining the relationship between the Soviet Union and its East European satellites. At a time when the Soviet economy was in deep trouble, the cost of maintaining a large army in Eastern Europe was becoming too high. Furthermore, Gorbachev needed loans and aid from the United States and Western Europe to help his policy of *perestroika*. While the Soviet Union still kept its hold on Eastern Europe, the chances of receiving that assistance were greatly reduced. To begin with, Gorbachev was reluctant to allow the satellites to go their own way. In 1986, he seemed to accept that the countries of Eastern Europe had the right to political independence, but he also seemed to insist that they still had to remain communist states.

It was not until 1988 that Gorbachev came down firmly in favour of allowing the establishment of independent, non-communist states in Eastern Europe. In his speeches, he stressed that the Soviet Union would not interfere in the internal politics of the East European countries and that it would no longer use its military muscle to prop up the communist governments of the region. The 'Brezhnev doctrine' justifying Soviet intervention abroad in order to defend communism was now replaced by the so-called 'Sinatra doctrine': 'You do it your way' (after the famous Frank Sinatra song *My Way*). At the end of 1988, Gorbachev announced that he would reduce the size of the Soviet armed forces in Eastern Europe. (In 1990 it was formally agreed that all Soviet forces would be pulled out of Eastern Europe over the following four years.)

Gorbachev's new thinking on Eastern Europe spelled the end for communism there. Having failed to win the confidence of the people, the communist governments held on to power only because the Soviet Union had in the past been prepared to prop them up militarily. Once they had lost the support of the Soviet leader, the communists were finished. The only questions remaining were when and how communism would end.

We cannot . . . fail to note the interest with which people follow new developments in the Soviet Union, how they listen to and read the speeches of Mikhail Gorbachev and compare his formulae with the deadly motionless in Czechoslovakia. The most experienced among us note that Soviet speeches are censored in the press.

A statement by Charter 77 in Czechoslovakia on the impact of Gorbachev in Eastern Europe.

# THE REVOLUTIONS OF 1989

## POLAND

*Free elections held in much of Eastern Europe in 1989 and 1990 resulted in massive defeats for the Communist Parties. In this photograph, taken at the end of 1990, Poles celebrate the election of Lech Walesa as the new Polish president.*

Poland was the first country in Eastern Europe to move from communism to democracy. The fact that Gorbachev lived up to his promises and did not intervene to save the Polish communists encouraged the rest of Eastern Europe to follow Poland's example.

Throughout the 1980s, Poland was racked by

strikes. The government of General Jaruzelski realized the urgent need to reform the economy. Yet without the support of the workers, the necessary reforms could only be put through by force possibly leading to civil war. Jaruzelski preferred more peaceful methods. In the summer of 1988, the Polish communists began holding talks with Lech Walesa and other leading trade-unionists. In their discussions, the communists gave way virtually entirely. In return for Solidarity's co-operation in the task of economic reform, they agreed to hold free elections to the Polish parliament and to allow Solidarity to put up its own candidates.

As expected, Solidarity won ninety-nine out of the 100 seats it contested in the Senate, and all the seats it contested in the Lower House in the election held in June 1989. Although Jaruzelski still tried to keep a communist government in power, he was soon obliged to give way to Solidarity. On 24 August 1989, Tadeusz Mazowiecki, one of Walesa's close colleagues from the days of the Gdansk strike in 1980, was sworn in as Poland's new, non-communist prime minister. Rather than intervening to prevent Mazowiecki's appointment, Gorbachev sent him a letter of congratulation. The next year, Lech Walesa was elected president of Poland.

# HUNGARY

In Poland, communist rule was overthrown by the Solidarity opposition. In Hungary, however, communism was destroyed by the Communist Party itself.

During the 1980s a substantial movement for economic and political reform had grown up within the Hungarian Communist Party. The 'reform-communists' recognized that drastic action was needed to get the country out of the economic chaos into which communism had brought it. In 1987, the reform-communists entered into an unofficial alliance with the leading anti-communist group, the Hungarian Democratic Forum. At a meeting of the Communist Party held the next year, the reformers voted the old communists out of power.

The reform-communists were playing a cunning game. They knew that communism was effectively finished in Hungary. By showing their support for reform and by joining forces with the opposition, they

Most of the estimated 2 million East Germans who flooded into West Berlin over the weekend simply walked the streets in quiet family groups, often with toddlers in pushchairs. They queued up at a bank to collect the 100 Deutschmarks 'greeting money' (about thirty-five pounds) offered to visiting East Germans by the West German government, and then they went, very cautiously, shopping. Generally, they bought one or two small items, perhaps some fresh fruit, a Western newspaper and toys for the children. Then, clasping their carrier-bags, they walked quietly back through the Wall, through the grey, deserted streets of East Berlin, home.

It is very difficult to describe the quality of this experience, because what they actually did was so stunningly ordinary. . . . Berliners walked the streets of Berlin. What could be more normal? And yet, what could be more fantastic!

A description of the scene as East Germans visit West Berlin following the opening of the Berlin Wall.

hoped to retain political influence in the future. During the course of 1989, the reform-communists agreed to make Hungary a democracy and to give up their hold on power. In June 1989, Imre Nagy, the hero of the 1956 Hungarian Revolution, was solemnly reburied in Budapest. (Following his execution in 1958, Nagy had been put in an unmarked grave.) Nagy's reburial, which was attended by an estimated 250,000 Hungarians, was a symbolic act which marked Hungary's acceptance of democracy.

In October 1989, the Hungarian Communist Party dissolved itself and declared that it would contest the forthcoming elections as the Socialist Party. Almost unnoticed outside the country, Hungary had ceased to be a communist state.

## EAST GERMANY

Even after the collapse of communist power in Poland and Hungary, few people expected the pace of change to quicken as it did, bringing down in rapid succession the communist governments in East Germany, Czechoslovakia, Romania and Bulgaria.

East Germany was one of the most repressive communist states. Its citizens were only permitted to visit other communist states and they were denied the right to travel to West Germany. The Berlin Wall was built in 1961 to stop East Germans escaping to the western half of the city.

In September 1989, Hungary, which by then was well on the way to ridding itself of communist rule, opened its border with Austria thus allowing free pasage out of the country for any who wanted to go. Immediately, tens of thousands of East Germans made their way to Hungary, crossed the border and moved to West Germany. When the East German government responded by stopping its citizens from visiting Hungary, East Germans took refuge in the grounds of the West German embassies in Prague and Warsaw.

The East German government gave way. It arranged for the refugees in Czechoslovakia and Poland to travel to West Germany on special trains. To try to prevent other East Germans joining them, the government banned all travel to neighbouring states.

The flight from East Germany was accompanied by widespread demonstrations against communist rule. To begin with, the government attempted to crush the demonstrations by force. Nevertheless, so many people were involved that it was impossible to stop them. In October 1989, at least 100,000 people demonstrated against communist rule in Leipzig. At the beginning of the next month, half a million East Germans joined in protests in East Berlin.

Under pressure from the streets, the East German government collapsed. On 18 October, Erich Honecker, who had ruled East Germany for almost twenty years, resigned. On 9 November, Honecker's successor agreed to let East Germans move freely through the Berlin Wall. The people immediately responded by starting to tear down this great symbol of communism that divided their city. The next day, the communist government announced it would hold free elections.

## CZECHOSLOVAKIA

The events in East Germany inspired the revolt against communism in Czechoslovakia. As in East Germany, massive demonstrations resulted in the collapse of the government. The protests were led by Vaclav Havel, one of the leaders of the Charter 77 movement, and were later joined by Alexander Dubcek, hero of the Prague Spring of 1968.

On 24 November 1989, the leaders of the communist government resigned, although the government

A few hours later, as Dubcek and Havel were giving a news conference in the Magic Lantern Theatre the news broke that [the entire communist leadership], which had spent all day closeted together in a crisis meeting had resigned. The two men fell into each other's arms. . . .

In the square, the people of Prague were catapulted into ecstasy, a joy heightened by the fear which had gone before. Taxis raced around the square with horns blaring, and a brass band in one corner oompahed out an end to four decades of communism. Nearby, a non-musician blew a trumpet, horribly out of tune.

The scene on 24 November 1989 when the news broke that the Czechoslovak communist leaders had resigned from power.

*Dissident and playwright, Vaclav Havel, gives a victory sign to his followers demonstrating in support of his appointment as Czechoslovakia's new president.*

**37**

itself remained in power. The following day about three-quarters of a million people demonstrated against communist rule in a stadium near Prague. In unison, they jangled their keys together: the sign for 'closing-time' in restaurants and bars in Czechoslovakia. Two days later, a general strike was called.

At first, the communist government considered using armed police against the demonstrators. The police chiefs made it clear, however, that they could not rely upon their officers and men to obey orders. With the protests growing and with no possibility of obtaining outside help against the demonstrators, the communists had no alternative except to resign from power.

In December 1989, a new non-communist government took over and parliament elected Vaclav Havel as Czechoslovakia's new president. The overthrow of communist rule in Czechoslovakia was achieved so peacefully that it soon became known as the 'Velvet Revolution'.

## ROMANIA, BULGARIA AND ALBANIA

*During his long rule as communist leader of Romania, Nicolae Ceausescu, shown here with his wife, Elena, made Romania one of the most repressive countries of Eastern Europe.*

Romania had been governed since 1975 by Nicolae Ceausescu. Ceausescu ruled in a harsh and corrupt manner. He appointed his wife and relatives to all the most important positions of government and lived in pampered luxury. His economic policies were so disastrous that Romania had the lowest standard of living in Europe. Nearly all basic goods had to be rationed and, in winter, no household was permitted more heat than a single bar on an electric fire.

Ceausescu ruthlessly suppressed any opposition to his rule. His security police, or *securitate*, hunted out critics of his policies. Opponents were jailed and sometimes they were even murdered. Nevertheless, because his government was

often critical of Soviet policy, Ceausescu was rewarded with aid and honours from the West. In 1978 he visited Great Britain and was even given an honorary knighthood. Only in the late 1980s did the western states begin to distance themselves from the Romanian leader and his policies.

Romania, however, could not remain isolated from the changes taking place elsewhere in Eastern Europe. In December 1989, demonstrations against Ceausescu's rule took place in the Romanian city of Timisoara. Ceausescu ordered the army and *securitate* to put down the protests. On 21 December a rally called by Ceausescu in the capital, Bucharest, to show support for communism turned into a riot. Throughout the city, demonstrators fought running battles with police and army units.

The next day, army generals, leading members of the Communist Party and the chiefs of the secret police mounted a *coup d'état* against Ceausescu and seized power. Some of the secret police, however, remained loyal to Ceausescu. For several days there was fierce shooting between the two sides on the streets of Bucharest which claimed dozens of lives.

*The army holds back demonstrators in the streets of Bucharest, the capital of Romania, on 21 December 1989. The next day, the army changed sides and toppled Ceausescu, the communist leader, from power.*

*Following his fall from power in November 1989, the communist leader of Bulgaria, Todor Zhivkov, was forced to stand trial on charges of corruption.*

Ceausescu and his wife were executed on Christmas Day 1989 following a mock trial which was then broadcast on television. The leaders of the *coup* against Ceausescu immediately declared the communist system abolished and announced that they would hold free and democratic elections to decide Romania's future.

Bulgaria gave up communism more slowly. In November 1989, the communist leader, Todor Zhivkov, who had ruled Bulgaria for thirty-five years, was arrested on charges of corruption. The new leadership announced that it would hold democratic elections in the middle of 1990. In the meantime, however, the communists remained in government and refused to share power with any of the new opposition parties. In the same year, communist power collapsed in Yugoslavia. The story of Yugoslavia is told in more detail later (pages 59-66).

Albania was the most isolated of the communist states. Its links with the outside world were few and it was friendly not towards the Soviet Union but instead towards China. In 1991, however, the Communist Party finally agreed in the face of mounting pressure to hold free elections.

## THE SOVIET UNION

Despite the collapse of communism in Eastern Europe, the Soviet Union remained a communist state. By not intervening to prop up the communist governments in Eastern Europe, Mikhail Gorbachev had made the move from communism to democracy possible there.

The pressure for change within the Soviet Union itself became irresistible. In 1990, the three Baltic republics, Estonia, Latvia and Lithuania, announced their independence from the Soviet Union.

Subsequent elections resulted in the Communist Party losing power in all three states. In other parts of the Soviet Union, the influence of the Communist Party also went into strong decline.

A particular problem faced by the Soviet Union was that it was the home of many peoples. These separate peoples became increasingly affected by nationalism and they demanded the right to establish their own independent states. Although Gorbachev was unwilling to allow the breakup of the Soviet Union, he agreed to a plan whereby the peoples of the Union would be allowed greater opportunity to decide on their own destinies.

Gorbachev's policies alarmed a number of the other communist leaders in the Soviet Union. They reckoned that Gorbachev's policies threatened the survival not only of communism but of the Soviet Union as well. In the early morning of 19 August 1991, the Soviet news agency, TASS, shocked the world by announcing that Gorbachev had been replaced as Soviet leader and that power had been taken by an Emergency Committee made up of his rivals. Tanks and troops were moved into the centre of Moscow and Leningrad. Gorbachev, on holiday in the Crimea, was placed under arrest.

The *coup* failed. Opposition on the streets of the capital and in the major Soviet cities was far greater than the plotters of the *coup* had anticipated. Furthermore, the army was not fully behind the rebellion. After barely two days, the *coup* leaders were forced to surrender.

The failure of the August *coup* resulted in a backlash against the Communist Party, which was thought by many people to have been behind the rebellion. Party offices were stormed and statues of Lenin, the founder of the Soviet Union, were toppled. In September, the Communist Party was banned by the Soviet parliament. At the end of the year, the Soviet Union itself came to an end. The USSR was replaced by a loose grouping of independent republics known as the Commonwealth of Independent States. Gorbachev himself was denied a place in the new structure and retired from politics.

Between 1989 and 1991 communism collapsed, therefore, entirely, both in Eastern Europe and in the Soviet Union. Not only did these momentous events spell the end of the Soviet Empire in Eastern Europe, but they led also to the end of the Soviet Union as well.

Clean water, clean air, clean government.

The truncheon — the beating heart of the Communist Party.

Long live the Communist Party — as a memory.

Whoever has to live in fear is not a free man.

Communists have palaces while our children lie among cockroaches in hospital.

Hurrah! Our teacher no longer has to lie — (signed) Schoolchildren.

Whoever has done evil has no right to govern.

A sample of wall graffiti from Czechoslovakia's Velvet Revolution.

# THE NEW DEMOCRACIES

## FREE ELECTIONS

The communists had never held fair and free elections anywhere in Eastern Europe. In a communist 'election' voters were given a ballot paper with only one name on it. If the voter approved the choice on the ballot paper he or she simply put it unmarked in a ballot box. If the voter disapproved of the candidate, he or she was supposed to write 'No' in full view of party officials in the polling station. Since people who made their disapproval known were often singled out afterwards for persecution, communist elections always resulted in massive victories for Communist Party candidates.

The collapse of communism in Eastern Europe was accompanied by promises that fair and free elections would be held as soon as possible. The peoples of Eastern Europe would now be given the chance to decide on the governments and political parties which would rule them in the future. Parliament rather than the Communist Party would be at the centre of power in each of the East European countries.

Throughout Eastern Europe political parties were rapidly established to contest the promised elections. No sooner were the revolutions complete than campaigning began in earnest. From the very start, the lead in the opinion polls in nearly all the East European countries was held by the parties which were the most strongly opposed to communism. These parties all promised to end political corruption, to establish genuine democracy, to abandon the communist economic system entirely, and to replace the state ownership of industry and agriculture with a market economy based on private ownership.

*In the first free election held in East Germany for over half a century, the voters were faced with a bewildering choice of parties and candidates.*

# THE UNIFICATION OF GERMANY

The first free election to be held in 1990 took place in East Germany in March. The Communist Party was decisively beaten by a coalition called the Alliance for Germany. The Alliance, however, was in favour not only of establishing a market economy as soon as pos-

*Ballot papers being counted in East Germany's first free election: victory in the election went to the party that promised the fastest reunification of Germany.*

sible, but also of joining East Germany with West Germany. Its success in the election was largely due to the fact that most East Germans wanted to live in a united German state.

Following the Alliance's victory in March, plans were immediately made to join together the two Germanys. In July, the separate East German currency, the Ostmark, was replaced by the West German Deutschmark. In October 1990, the East German state was abolished and Germany was reunified. Thus the first freely elected East German government was also East Germany's last.

# DEMOCRATIC GOVERNMENT IN EASTERN EUROPE

Elections held in Hungary and Czechoslovakia in March and June 1990, also resulted in victories for anti-communist parties. In Hungary the election was won by the Hungarian Democratic Forum. The leadership of the Forum consisted of politicians who had previously played a major role in forcing the Hungarian communists to give up power. In Czechoslovakia, well over half the seats in the parliament were won by the Civic Forum, which had led the struggle against communist rule in Czechoslovakia in November 1989.

In Romania and Bulgaria, however, the communists were able to hold on to power. In Romania, the National Salvation Front, which had taken power immediately after the fall of Nicolae Ceausescu, comprised a large number of leading Communist Party officials. These Romanian communists now all announced that they had seen the error of their ways and had become democrats.

In the election campaign, however, the National Salvation Front did not hold back from using violent methods. It had doubled the wages of the country's coalminers, and now used them as a private army to attack the headquarters of other political parties. At the same time, the Front claimed that transferring industry from state ownership to private ownership, as the rival political parties wanted to do, would lead to massive unemployment. Having terrified the opposition parties by its use of force and having frightened the voters by its talk of unemployment, the Front held a rigged election. It is thought that as many as a million fraudulent votes were put into the ballot boxes.

Not surprisingly, the National Salvation Front won a landslide victory in the election, obtaining over two-thirds of the seats in the Romanian parliament. Ion Iliescu, a former close supporter of Nicolae Ceausescu, won 85 per cent of the vote for the office of president. When demonstrators protested in June 1990 at the methods used by the Front, Iliescu sent in his own private army of miners to disperse them. For two days, the miners terrorized the streets of the Romanian capital, Bucharest. Protests from western politicans forced the government to hold back in future from using fraud and violence. New parliamentary elections, held in September 1992, were conducted more fairly and the vote received by the National Salvation Front fell to under 40 per cent.

In Bulgaria, elections held in June 1990 were won by the communists, now renamed the Bulgarian Socialist Party. The communists achieved their victory by methods similar to those used in Romania by the National Salvation Front. The Bulgarian communists frightened the voters by claiming that the other political parties, if they won the election, would stop paying

[The Party] impressed upon voters that if they wanted to hang on to their social security, free education, free medical care etc they had better stay with the socialists [until February 1990, the communists]. It was there to read in the Bulgarian Socialist Party's manifesto — in capital letters — the terrible consequences of voting for the opposition: 'mass unemployment, exorbitant prices, irresistible inflation, outflow of an enormous portion of the national income, fast sale of the few good things Bulgaria has'; still more persuasive, though, might be a well-timed visit from a local official bringing your monthly pension and insinuating that this might be your last.

An example of election campaigning in Bulgaria in 1990.

*In June 1990, when students protested against the continued presence of a large number of former communists in the new Romanian government, President Iliescu ordered his own private army of miners to break up the demonstration.*

pensions and other benefits. Communist Party officials used their influence in the countryside to prevent the other parties from campaigning.

As in Romania, there was considerable dissatisfaction about the ways used by the Bulgarian communists to win the election. A general strike and demonstrations in the capital, Sofia, forced the communists to agree to fresh elections. In October 1991, the communists were narrowly defeated by the opposition Union of Democratic Forces which then formed the new government.

Following the elections of 1990, therefore, communist power in Eastern Europe was replaced by a system which was more democratic. Instead of there being one political party, which everybody had to vote for, a number of different parties competed for power and for the people's votes. In a few places, as in Bulgaria and Romania, the move from communism to democracy was not accomplished without difficulties on account of the strong resistance shown by the former Communist Parties. Even in these countries, however, genuinely fair and free elections were eventually held.

Nevertheless, it was clear even at the time of the elections that a strong democratic system in Eastern Europe would not be easy to establish. The countries of Eastern Europe faced enormous social, economic and political problems, the most serious of which were rising unemployment, nationalism and 'neo-communism'. Unless managed properly, these problems could be sufficiently serious to jeopardize democracy in the countries of Eastern Europe.

# MOVING TO THE MARKET

## MARKETIZATION

*A Soviet oil installation in Latvia. When the Soviet Union put up the price of its oil exports in 1990, the countries of Eastern Europe experienced a sudden and unwelcome shock to their economies.*

The communist economies in Eastern Europe had the following features: First, all industry and most agriculture was state owned. Private ownership was forbidden, and therefore nearly everybody worked for the state. Secondly, the communist economies were 'planned economies'. In each branch of industry and agriculture, production and priorities were established on the basis of plans drawn up jointly by government ministers, party officials and factory managers.

Most of the new governments which took power after the elections of 1990 were committed to replacing state ownership and planning with a market economy. In a market economy (the type of economic system which is normal in, for example, Western Europe and North America) most industry and agriculture is privately owned, and businesses set their own priorities, production targets and prices.

The problem was, however, that the move from a state controlled economy to a private, market economy had never been attempted before anywhere in the world. Although some individual businesses in Western Europe had been returned from state control to private ownership through the process known as 'privatization', never before had entire economies been privatized.

In addition, the East European countries had always depended heavily upon the Soviet Union for cheap oil in return for which they exported manufactured goods. In 1990, however, the Soviet Union put up the price of the oil it sent abroad and cut back on its imports from Eastern Europe. Thus, the countries of Eastern Europe began the reform of their economies at a time when they faced a major crisis in their international trade.

## PRICES, SUBSIDIES AND PRIVATIZATION

'Marketization', as the process of moving to a market economy is sometimes known, involved three stages, all of which were fraught with difficulties.

The first stage was 'price-liberalization'. Instead of the prices of goods being fixed by officials as part of the country's economic plan, factory managers were now allowed to decide how much they wanted to charge for their goods. Most decided to put up their prices with the result that the rate of inflation increased rapidly. Price-liberalization in Czechoslovakia at the start of 1991 led immediately to a monthly inflation rate of over 25 per cent.

Wages in Eastern Europe seldom kept pace with inflation, resulting in great hardship. Many goods, such as meat or clothing, became too expensive to buy. After price-liberalization, a pair of shoes often cost as much in Eastern Europe as a whole month's salary. Nevertheless, as the population stopped purchasing anything other than essential goods, factory

The huge sums spent on the direct subsidization of the various sectors of the national economy markedly distort the value judgement of the market, disorient the development of policy, and necessitate the collection of irrationally large sums in taxes. The government is determined to introduce considerable cuts in subsidies. . . . In 1991 the government will reduce the amount of state subsidies by 50 billion forints [$1000,000,000].

This economic programme was announced by the Hungarian government in September 1990.

*The removal of subsidies from basic foodstuffs in Czechoslovakia at the start of 1991 caused some prices to rise by as much as 100 per cent. Price-liberalization proved especially hard for pensioners.*

managers were soon forced to cut their prices. The result was that the inflation rate steadied during 1991-92 and, in Czechoslovakia, fell back to 2-3 per cent a month.

The second stage of marketization proved more difficult. In the past, the communist governments had kept loss-making industries going by giving them special grants or subsidies. This was particularly the case with steel making and engineering, two branches of industry which employed tens of millions of East Europeans.

In large parts of Eastern Europe, the new democratic governments began to withdraw these subsidies. The politicians argued that money should not be spent supporting industries which were unprofitable. Having lost their government subsidies, many factories either closed or cut back their production. Industrial output in Eastern Europe fell dramatically therefore after 1990. As a consequence, the workforce throughout the region faced rising unemployment and short-term working. In 1991, unemployment reached 300,000 in Hungary and 2 million in Poland. Even in the former East Germany, where industry received help from West German business, unemployment grew to 3 million, about a third of the workforce.

The third stage of marketization was to privatize the economy by converting state-owned factories and industries into privately-owned enterprises. Eastern Europe lacked, however, sufficient wealthy people with enough spare money to buy factories from the state. At the same time, the governments of Eastern Europe were often reluctant to allow foreign companies to acquire state-owned enterprises. The new governments of Eastern Europe reckoned that businesses owned abroad would not always work in the best interests of East Europeans.

One of the most popular solutions followed in Eastern Europe was to sell off shares in large state industries to employees and the general public. Small businesses, like shops and restaurants which had previously been state owned, were sold at auctions to the highest bidder. The centres of the major cities of Eastern Europe soon filled with new bars, pizza parlours and boutiques.

Few Eastern Europeans, however, had sufficient money of their own either to purchase many shares or to buy a business at an auction. As a result, the pace of privatization had to proceed much more slowly than the governments in Eastern Europe would have liked. Three years after the collapse of communism in Hungary, 85 per cent of the country's economy was therefore still state owned. In Poland, the ambitious start made in 1991 to sell off 400 state industries had to be drastically cut back on account of the lack of money for investment in industry.

Even those businesses which were privatized seemed sometimes to have fallen into the wrong hands. The wealthiest people in Eastern Europe were often those who had done well under communism by occupying leading posts in the Party and by engaging in corruption. To ordinary East Europeans, it seemed unfair that these former communists should now be able to buy up so many of the shares and businesses that were for sale.

Government subsidies for all commodities except basic staple foods, heating, electricity and rents were removed on 1 November 1990, and their prices 'liberalized' as part of the first stage of the economic reform programme. The first stage of price-liberalization was principally intended to permit enterprises to set prices to cover the true costs of production. . . . Liberalization resulted in retail price increases of between 100-300 per cent for the majority of consumer goods affected.

The effect of price-liberalization and inflation in Romania.

From Economist Intelligence Unit, *Country Report Romania* (1991).

## DISILLUSIONMENT

Most East Europeans had believed that marketization of the economy would result in increased wealth and prosperity. They had imagined that replacing the

*After reunification, many inefficient factories were closed down in the former East Germany. As a consequence, workers lost their jobs and unemployment rose to almost 35 per cent of the work force. This picture shows an unemployment office in former East Germany in 1994.*

communist economic system with a market economy would soon make their countries as rich as those in Western Europe.

Inflation, unemployment and the slow pace of privatization dashed these hopes. Although the economies of Poland, Hungary and the Czech Republic (as the western part of Czechoslovakia became known in 1993, see page 55) showed strong improvement in the early 1990s, some East Europeans began to feel that they had been let down by the newly-elected governments of their country. Others began to look around for scapegoats and blamed minorities such as Jews and Gypsies for damaging the economies of Eastern Europe.

# NATIONALISM

## NATIONS AND NATIONALISM IN EASTERN EUROPE

Nationalism is the belief that the world is organized into nations, that everybody belongs to a nation and that the best type of political arrangement is where each nation has its own state in which to live. Sometimes, however, nationalism can lead to intolerance. This is particularly the case when one nation believes itself to be superior to another, or when members of one nation dispute the right of another, smaller nation to live and dwell in the same state as themselves.

Eastern Europe consists mainly of nation states, where one nation makes up almost the entire population of the state. Nevertheless, throughout Eastern Europe there are also a substantial number of national minorities. These are people who do not

*Despite their colourful costumes, Gypsies (Roma), like these in Hungary, are the poorest part of the population of Eastern Europe. Many have also been the victims of racist attacks by groups of skinheads and neo-Nazis.*

share the same language, religion or culture with the majority population of the state.

One of the largest minority groups in Eastern Europe is Gypsies. In Poland, Hungary, Czechoslovakia and Romania, there are as many as 2 or even 3 million Gypsies. (Reliable figures are still impossible to obtain.) Romania has a large Hungarian minority of 1.6 million; Poland has several hundred thousand Germans; and Bulgaria has a population of almost a million Turks.

Some of the states of Eastern Europe were not nation states but multinational states. None was as complex as the Soviet Union in which several hundred different nations lived. Czechoslovakia, however, was also a multinational state and the home of 10 million Czechs, 5 million Slovaks and 700,000 Hungarians. Yugoslavia (the recent history of which will be dealt with more fully on pages 59-66) was the home of six different national groups.

## COMMUNISM AND NATIONALISM

The communist governments of Eastern Europe had tried to suppress national feelings. They had argued that the peoples of the region should feel themselves first and foremost to be communists. Under the communist governments of Eastern Europe, the statues of national heroes were frequently replaced with statues of Lenin, the founder of the Soviet Union, and street names honoured communist champions. The emblems in the centre of each national flag and the symbol of the red star reminded East Europeans that they were also members of an international communist community.

On occasions, however, the communists showed themselves ready to exploit nationalism and national intolerance for political purposes. In order to explain economic failure, the communists in the 1940s and 50s regularly blamed the Jews. As late as the 1980s the government in Romania accused Jews of murdering Christian children. In order to frighten the population into obedience, the Romanian communists also claimed that the Hungarians in Romania were plotting to take away a part of Romania and join it to Hungary.

With the overthrow of communism in 1989, East Europeans set about recovering and rediscovering their national past. They ripped out the communist emblems from the centre of their national flags, pulled down the statues of Lenin, and changed the street names

I want my fellow-Germans to feel equal citizens in Poland, have access to German culture, feel safe. I dream that I may sit in my garden at night and sing German songs with my friends without stones being thrown on us.

One of the German minority of several hundred thousand persons living in Poland speaks of his hopes.

back to what they had been before the communists had taken power. New national heroes were proclaimed: the leaders of the 1956 Hungarian Revolution, of the Prague Spring and of Polish Solidarity.

With these changes, the peoples of Eastern Europe were once again able to feel proud of belonging to their separate nations. No longer obliged to think of themselves as communists first and as Hungarians, Poles or Czechs only second, they could now express their loyalty to the nation to which they belonged.

*Following the collapse of communism, roads were renamed in much of Eastern Europe. In this picture, Budapest street names recalling Lenin and the Russian Revolution of 1917 have been replaced.*

Within a short time, however, national pride gave way to national intolerance. This was partly due to the way the communists had exploited nationalism in the past as a way of making scapegoats. Nevertheless, the new mood also owed much to the frustration felt by many East Europeans that the recent economic changes had not brought the prosperity that they had expected.

National intolerance was most usually shown in attitudes towards minorities. Within a few months of the Romanian Revolution of 1989, Romanian journalists and politicians began criticizing the Hungarian minority in Romania on account of its alleged 'arrogance'. In March 1990, mobs of Romanian peasants attacked Hungarians in the city of Tirgu Mures, killing at least six of them.

Gypsies and Jews were also among the first targets of national intolerance. In 1990, gangs of skinheads roamed several cities in Czechoslovakia hunting out and beating up Gypsies. In Romania, one of the most popular newspapers ran regular features on the way the country was being 'polluted' not just by Hungarians but by Jews and Gypsies as well.

In East Germany and Czechoslovakia, considerable violence was shown towards guest workers. The guest workers came mainly from Third World countries and had been recruited by the communists to work in the more badly-paid jobs. After the revolution in Czechoslovakia, many of the country's guest workers, mostly Vietnamese, were made to return home. In eastern Germany in 1992, youths firebombed hostels for

We can no longer ignore the fact that there are certain genetic reasons for this deterioration. We must understand that we have lived for too long a time with disadvantaged strata and groups where natural selection could not operate. Society must now support the strong families that are fit for life and organized for work and performance.

A leading Hungarian politician explaining in 1992 the reasons for what he sees as the 'sickness' in Hungarian society. His comments are a coded attack on Hungary's Gypsy population.

guest workers in order to force them to leave the country. Jewish cemeteries were vandalized. In 1993 in Bulgaria there was also a sharp increase in the number of reported attacks on Gypsies.

The spread of national intolerance also affected Russia. In elections held in December 1993 for the new Russian parliament, the State Duma, the Liberal Democrats emerged as the largest party with almost a quarter of the vote. Despite their name, the Liberal Democrats, headed by Vladimir Zhirinovsky, were an extreme right-wing party committed to the expansion of Russia's borders and to ridding the country of 'foreign' influences.

*In 1992 there were a number of demonstrations and attacks on foreigners in former East German towns. A Turkish woman and two of her granddaughters died in a fire at this house in Moellen after it was attacked by neo-Nazis. Sympathetic Germans lit candles and laid wreaths on the pavement outside.*

## BREAKING UP IN EASTERN EUROPE

The strong growth of nationalism in Eastern Europe brought an end to the region's multinational states. Following the failed *coup* in August 1991, the Soviet Union disintegrated. It was replaced by separate republics all of which were organized as independent nation states. However, the mix of peoples in the former Soviet Union meant that most of the new states contained substantial minority populations. In Georgia and Azerbaijan, fighting erupted between the different national groups. In Estonia, the Russian minority, which amounted to a third of Estonia's population, was denied the right to participate in the Estonian elections held in 1992.

In Chechnya, a small republic in the Russian Federation, the problem was different. In late 1994 Chechnya declared its desire for independence from the Federation. The Russian president, Boris Yeltsin, was not prepared to let it go and in December sent his troops in to remove the government. The nationalist Chechen fighters defended their capital, Grozny, vigorously against the much larger and better equipped Russian army, but were forced to abandon it in early

February 1995 and take to the surrounding country-side. It is possible that other national minorities in Russia will, over the next few years, seek independence from Moscow.

In 1991, the multinational state of Yugoslavia also fell apart. Fierce fighting ensued between Serbs, Croats and Bosnian Muslims (see pages 59-66).

The breakup of Czechoslovakia happened more peacefully. Although they speak languages that are closely related, Czechs and Slovaks always felt themselves to be different from one another. Both peoples also distrusted each other. Czechs believed Slovaks to be less educated and unsophisticated; Slovaks thought Czechs to be proud and disdainful. Economic differences sharpened this distrust. Slovakia had always been the poorer part of Czechoslovakia and Slovaks depended on money coming from the Czech lands to keep their industry going. Czechs, however, resented the way that their resources were used to prop up the Slovak economy.

Elections held in Czechoslovakia in 1992 exposed these differences and, although opinion polls showed that a majority of neither Czechs nor Slovaks wanted Czechoslovakia to break up, an agreement over economic policy could not be reached. At the end of 1992, Czechoslovakia was officially dissolved. It was replaced by two independent nation states: the Czech Republic and Slovakia. The breakup of Czechoslovakia was achieved without violence, but worries for the future remained.

*In 1991, the former Soviet republic of Georgia declared its independence. Within a few months, however, the new country had dissolved into civil war. The president was overthrown in a military coup and fighting broke out between Georgians and some of the countries ethnic minorities.*

# THE RISE OF NEO-COMMUNISM

## COMMUNIST INFLUENCE

*Soviet premier (1983-84) Yuri Andropov's membership card for the Communist Party. Former Communist Party members have often claimed that party membership was like a driving licence: a qualification necessary for personal progress.*

Even after the revolutions of 1989 and their defeat in the elections held in 1990, many communists were not prepared to give up the power and influence that they had once enjoyed. A large number retained the positions that they had occupied before 1989 and refused to resign their posts. Others used money which they had acquired while in office to buy up businesses. A few, on account of their skills in administration and finance, continued to be employed at the highest level of government.

The success with which many former communists managed to retain influence led to resentment in Eastern Europe. Despite the move from communism to democracy, it seemed that too many faces at the top remained the same. Neo-communism, the reappearance of former communists in important positions in the country, was a description frequently used in the early 1990s to describe the political situation in a large part of Eastern Europe.

Many former communists claimed that they had joined the Communist Party and supported the communist government because they had no alternative. Had they refused, their families might have suffered. Others pointed out that until 1989 membership of the Communist Party had often been necessary for any sort of promotion.

Although to a large extent

ПАРТИЙНЫЙ БИЛЕТ
№ 00000017
Фамилия *Андропов*
Имя *Юрий*
Отчество *Владимирович*
Год рождения 1914
Время вступления в партию *февраль 1939 г.*
Наименование партийного органа, выдавшего билет
*Партком*
*КГБ при Совете Министров СССР*

Дата выдачи „ 2 " *марта* 1973 г.

УПЛАТА ЧЛЕНСКИХ
19.73 год

| Месяц | Месячный заработок | Сумма взноса |
|---|---|---|
| Январь | | |
| Февраль | | |
| Март | 800 | 24 |
| Апрель | 800 | 24 |
| Май | 800 | 24 |
| Июнь | 800 | 24 |
| Июль | 800 | 24 |
| Август | 800 | 24 |
| Сентябрь | 800 | 24 |
| Октябрь | 800 | 24 |
| Ноябрь | 800 | 24 |
| Декабрь | 800 | 24 |

justified, these claims did not altogether convince many East Europeans. They wanted to know precisely what the 'old faces at the top' had been doing before 1989 and the extent to which they had actively supported the communist governments which were then in power.

In Czechoslovakia and East Germany, interest centred in particular on the files of the former secret police. These contained much information on the activities of former communists. Often the files included details of corrupt practices, and they named people who had been working behind the scenes for the police.

Examination of the files proved embarrassing for some of the new, democratically-elected politicians in Eastern Europe. In 1990, the first non-communist prime minister of East Germany and several of his ministers had to resign following accusations that they had worked for the secret police. In Czechoslovakia, several prominent MPs and former leading dissidents were exposed in 1991 as having been police informers.

## OLD COMMUNISTS

In several East European countries, some former communists were able to earn themselves popularity by making extreme nationalist statements. By pandering to people's worst instincts, the ex-communists hoped to draw public attention away from their disreputable pasts.

In Romania, therefore, the communists who took power after the revolution of 1989 publicly supported organizations which had been responsible for the some of the worst nationalist violence committed against Romania's Hungarians in 1990. Following elections held in Romania in 1992, the government party went into coalition with two of the country's most extreme nationalist parties. In Slovakia, the politician who led the country to independence was a former communist youth leader and police informer. In his speeches he frequently took up an intolerant position towards Slovakia's Gypsy and Hungarian minorities.

Elsewhere, communists were able to retain influence by declaring that the old communist system was preferable to the new market economy. In Bulgaria, the Communist Party (renamed the Bulgarian Socialist Party) remained throughout the early 1990s the second largest party. After 1992, the opposition of the Bulgarian socialists to market reforms forced the government to adopt a much

In January 1990, Meciar started his administration with a house cleaning, dismissing most of the nation's police chiefs. Within six months, however, he had restored them all to power.

Within the Interior Ministry building itself, Meciar fired only seven of the forty-two officials who had worked with the communist secret police.

(Vladimir Meciar, who later became the first prime minister of independent Slovakia, held the office of minister of the interior after the 1989 revolution in Czechoslovakia.)

From *East European Reporter* (January/February 1992).

slower privatization programme. In Russia, the former communists who dominated the Russian parliament, or Congress of People's Deputies, consistently refused to support the market reforms introduced by the Russian president, Boris Yeltsin. In October 1993, Yeltsin took the drastic step of closing down the Russian parliament and ordering new elections. When the communists in the parliament refused to disperse, Yeltsin had the parliament building occupied by armed troops.

In a number of countries, former communists were able to regain influence by moderating their policies. Discarding both their communist beliefs and neo-communist techniques, former communists in Hungary adopted moderate policies similar to those followed by social democrat parties in Western Europe. Hungary's ex-communists, renamed the Hungarian Socialist Party, stressed that while they were still committed to market reforms they also wanted to remove many of the social injustices caused by the recent economic changes in Eastern Europe. In elections held in May 1994, the Hungarian Socialist Party received a majority of votes cast and formed the new government. In elections held in Lithuania in October 1992 and in Poland in September 1993, former communists who had now become social democrats also recorded strong successes at the polls.

*This photograph shows the burning Russian parliament building in Moscow in October 1993. It was shelled by troops loyal to Boris Yeltsin during its occupation by former communists who opposed his policies.*

# CIVIL WAR

## ORIGINS OF THE WAR IN YUGOSLAVIA

For a long time Yugoslavia seemed to disprove the idea that communist states were invariably drab, poverty-stricken and brutally run. The people of Yugoslavia, at least in the cities, seemed prosperous; although a secret police operated, there were few political prisoners; and, unlike most other Eastern Europeans, Yugoslavs could travel abroad to Western Europe.

In 1991, however, just as Yugoslavia began to move from communism to democracy, the country dissolved into civil war. Yugoslavia's peaceful cities were rapidly transformed into islands of desolation where thousands of refugees sought shelter from murder, rape and 'ethnic cleansing'.

The collapse of Yugoslavia and the outbreak of civil war owed much to the wider problems which have been shown in the last three chapters as troubling nearly all of Eastern Europe. These problems may be summed up as the economic difficulties caused by marketization, growing national intolerance, and neo-communism. In Yugoslavia, these problems fed upon each other and became so intertwined as to lead to a bloody conflict.

Like the Soviet Union and Czechoslovakia, Yugoslavia was a multinational state and was the home of six separate national groups: Serbs, Croats, Slovenes, Macedonians, Bosnian Muslims and

| Nationality | Percentage of Population of Yugoslavia |
|---|---|
| Serbs | 40 |
| Croats | 20 |
| Slovenes | 8 |
| Albanians | 7.7 |
| Muslims | 9 |
| Macedonians | 2.6 |
| Others | 12.7 |
| (*Source:* 1981 census) | |

Albanians. Each of these separate nationalities has its own distinctive history and culture as well as its own special sense of national pride and, more often than not, its own language.

Following the communist take-over in 1945, Yugoslavia had been made into a federation of six republics: Serbia, Croatia, Slovenia, Macedonia, Bosnia-Herzegovina and Montenegro. Although considerable power was still held by the central, federal government in Belgrade, each of the six republics had been allowed a measure of self-government.

The federal structure of Yugoslavia was intended to allow each of the country's national groups to feel that they had their own state, even though they still remained a part of multinational Yugoslavia. The problem was that the various nationalities did not all live in single compact groups but in splinters. Thus, 10 per cent of the population of Croatia was Serb and there were also large Albanian and Hungarian minorities in Serbia. Bosnia-Herzegovina itself was a complete hotch-potch where no one nation formed the majority.

## SERBIA AND MILOSEVIC

Between 1945 and 1980, Yugoslavia was ruled by Marshal Tito. As one of the leaders of the guerrilla movement in the Second World War, when Yugoslavia had been overrun by the Germans and Italians, Tito held enormous prestige among ordinary Yugoslavs. His personality and occasional ruthlessness helped keep Yugoslavia together.

After Tito's death in 1980, resentments came to the surface and pitted Yugoslavia's national groups against one another. Economic difficulties proved a major cause of dissatisfaction. Slovenes and Croats were increasingly convinced that their more efficient industry and agriculture were being used to pay for 'lazy' Serbs, Montenegrins and Macedonians.

During the 1970s and 80s, as Tito and his successors began experimenting with marketization, there was a rapid growth in inflation and unemployment. By the end of the 1980s the inflation rate had reached 2,000 per cent a year and almost a fifth of the workforce was jobless. During the decade 1980-90, the spending power of Yugoslavs fell by as much as a half. The calamitous condition of the Yugoslav economy worsened relations

*Serbian leader Slobodan Milosevic's use of nationalist slogans worsened the political tension between the Serbs and the other nationalities of Yugoslavia.*

between the wealthier Slovenes and Croats and the poorer peoples of Yugoslavia.

Historically, the Serbs had always regarded Serbia as being the most important state in Yugoslavia. Many Serbs, however, believed that the federation of six republics had been deliberately designed to reduce Serbian influence. Some Serbs also disliked the way Tito had given the Albanian minority living in Kosovo in Serbia special privileges including the right to have its own mini-parliament. With Tito's death they saw an opportunity to readjust the balance of power in Yugoslavia to their own advantage.

In 1986 Slobodan Milosevic was appointed president of Serbia. Although for most of his life a convinced communist, Milosevic had realized by 1989 that communism was finished in Eastern Europe. Accordingly, he changed his views entirely and began to speak out no longer as a communist but as a Serbian nationalist.

Milosevic's tactic of switching from communism to nationalism was typical of the methods used elsewhere in Eastern Europe by other neo-communist leaders. Unlike these others, however, Milosevic was ready to push his extremist brand of nationalism to the point of civil war. Appealing to Serbian nationalism, Milosevic pushed hard for a restoration of Serbian power and influence in Yugoslavia. In 1989, the parliament of the Serbian republic removed the special privileges of the Albanians of Kosovo. Albanian schools in Kosovo were closed down and 15,000 Albanian civil servants were dismissed.

Having broken the power of the non-Serb nationalities in Serbia itself, Milosevic then turned his attention to Yugoslavia as a whole. In 1989 he took control of the presidential council, the highest organ of government in Yugoslavia.

Croat and Slovene politicians feared that their own republics would soon be taken over by Serbia. In order to demonstrate how different they were to Milosevic, the Croat and Slovene politicians organized free elections. The result was the election in both Slovenia and Croatia of parliaments committed to making the two republics into completely independent states.

## WAR IN CROATIA

In June 1991 Slovenia and Croatia declared themselves to be fully independent. Early the next year, two

*During the conflict in Bosnia-Herzegovina Muslim civilians were frequently interned by the Serb forces in detention camps, some of which were administered with extreme brutality. The camp shown in this photograph is housed in a former farm building.*

other republics, Bosnia-Herzegovina and Macedonia, announced their own independence.

Milosevic and Serbia's other hardline politicians were ready to let Slovenia go. After a brief bout of fighting, the Serbian-led Yugoslav army evacuated the new state. Croatia, however, was quite another matter. The republic of Croatia contained a large Serbian population. It was Milosevic's intention to seize for Serbia the territories in which these Serbs lived even though they were parts of Croatia. Since the Croatian government was not prepared to surrender any of its territory, war was unavoidable. Fighting between Serbian and Croatian forces began in the summer of 1991. Serbian troops rapidly gained the upper hand occupying roughly a third of Croatian territory.

The conflict between Serbs and Croats was fought with an almost unbelievable brutality. Both sides relied on untrained troops and ill-disciplined volunteers who tortured and looted their way through the countryside. A particular feature of the war in Croatia was ethnic cleansing. Ethnic cleansing meant evicting from an area all those of a different national origin. Ethnic cleansing was practised mainly by the Serbian

*In April 1992, Sarajevo, the capital city of Bosnia-Herzegovina, was besieged by Serb forces. From their positions in the hills around Sarajevo, Serb snipers and artillery fired down on the city's inhabitants.*

We all come from Kozarac, a small Muslim town in northern Bosnia. The Serbs occupied our town, killing, robbing and raping. Then they blew up our homes, leaving us only with what we carry ourselves.

A Muslim refugee's story of ethnic cleansing, November 1992.

forces. In villages captured by Serb troops, the Croat population was made to leave at gunpoint and their homes were given over to Serbian families.

In January 1992 the Serbian leaders agreed to a cease-fire negotiated by representatives of the European Community and United Nations. The United Nations sent 14,000 troops into Croatia to keep the peace and to hold the two armies apart. In the following weeks the European Community recognized Slovenia, Croatia and Bosnia as fully independent states.

## WAR IN BOSNIA-HERZEGOVINA

In the spring of 1992, Milosevic turned his attention to Bosnia-Herzegovina. Serbian troops took over the eastern and northern portions of the republic where the Serbs of Bosnia-Herzegovina were mainly located. Croatian forces meanwhile advanced from the west to protect the republic's Croatian population. In the areas they occupied, the Serbian army continued with its policy of ethnic cleansing. Muslims and Croats who had lived for generations with Serbs in mixed communities were driven from their homes.

During the course of 1992-93, over a million Bosnians were made homeless and became refugees. Several hundreds of thousands were also interned in concentration camps which were administered with extreme brutality by the Serbian forces. Many thousands of civilians were killed or died of starvation in these camps.

*Radovan Karadzic, leader of the Bosnian Serbs, is believed to have approved many of the atrocities committed by the Serb forces in Bosnia-Herzegovina.*

The conflict in Bosnia-Herzegovina was waged with an even greater ferocity than the earlier war in Croatia. The capital of Bosnia-Herzegovina, Sarajevo, which was held by Muslim forces, was subject to a continuous bombardment from Serbian positions in the surrounding hills. Cities full of refugees were also the frequent target of Serbian snipers and artillery. Prisoners captured by the Serbian forces were often tortured and the women raped.

As the war continued during 1992 and 1993, atrocities were regularly committed by all sides and no longer by just the Serbs. The Croats began ethnic cleansing in the parts of Bosnia which their forces occupied. The resistance of Bosnian Muslims to attacks by both Serbs and Croats sometimes led them, too, to deliberately massacre civilians.

Both the United Nations and the European Community were reluctant to take military action to halt the atrocities. They preferred to try and negotiate a settlement rather than to impose one by force. Only in the winter of 1992 were United Nations forces sent into Bosnia-Herzegovina to guard relief supplies. By this time the fighting in the former Yugoslavia had created over 4 million refugees and had claimed at least 50,000 lives.

Negotiations over Bosnia-Herzegovina failed, however, to yield a solution. By 1993 it had been accepted that Bosnia-Herzegovina would have to be divided up into two separate states: one for the Serbs; the other for the Croats and Muslims. Disputes over where the border between the two states should run prompted fresh outbreaks of fighting and ethnic cleansing throughout 1993 and 1994.

## CIVIL WAR IN EASTERN EUROPE?

Yugoslavia was not the only multinational state in Eastern Europe to witness an upsurge in national intolerance. During the early 1990s worry was felt that other parts of Eastern Europe might dissolve into inner turmoil and civil war.

In the former Soviet Union, fighting intensified during the early 1990s between Armenians and Azeris in Azerbaijan and erupted between Georgians and Abkhazis in Georgia. In Moldova, which neighbours Romania and which was also once a part of the Soviet Union, civil war briefly broke out in 1991 between the majority Romanian population and the minority Russian population.

The growth of extremist nationalism in Romania and Slovakia in the early 1990s led to tension in both states between the majority Romanian and Slovak populations and their Hungarian minorities. In neither country, however, did it seem likely that these tensions would actually result in widespread violence.

Fears, however, were felt for the republic of Macedonia, which until 1992 had been a part of Yugoslavia and which remained a possible victim of Serbian aggression. If Macedonia, the population of which is divided between Macedonians and Albanians, was drawn into the fighting in the former Yugoslavia, the war might draw in the neighbouring countries of Albania, Bulgaria and Greece. As it is, tension between Greece and Macedonia, caused in part by Macedonia's use of allegedly Greek national symbols, resulted in 1992 in Greece closing its border with Macedonia and stopping the movement of commercial traffic. The Greek government's objections served also to delay until 1993 the European Community's recognition of Macedonia as an independent state.

Although it is highly improbable that all of Eastern Europe could fall victim to civil war, enough potential flashpoints remain to give cause for concern. The weak international response to the conflict in the former Yugoslavia might also encourage nationalist politicians elsewhere in Eastern Europe to embark upon their own wars of aggression.

*This map shows the internal divisions of Yugoslavia before the outbreak of civil war and the main areas of conflict since the fighting began.*

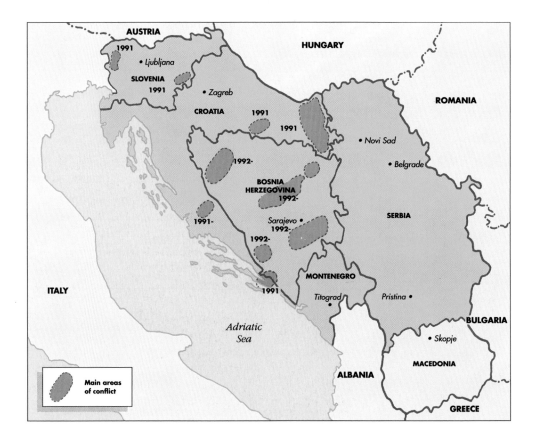

# EASTERN AND WESTERN EUROPE

## WESTERN EUROPE AND THE REVOLUTIONS IN EASTERN EUROPE

T he governments of Western Europe and of the United States welcomed the collapse of communism. Not only were the peoples of Eastern Europe no longer suffering under repressive governments but also the possibility of war breaking out between the two halves of Europe was dramatically reduced. As a consequence, the money previously

*The extent of new western investment in Eastern Europe is symbolized by the spread of McDonald's restaurants from Moscow to Budapest to Belgrade. This one is in Gdansk, in Poland.*

spent on armies and weapons in Western Europe and the United States could be used for other, more peaceful, purposes. Politicians began talking enthusiastically of the 'peace dividend' — the money which could be saved now that the Cold War was over.

During the early 1990s, these hopes gradually gave way to more cautious assessments. The major difficulties faced by the East European economies in moving to the market became increasingly obvious. Even the stronger Hungarian, Polish and Czech economies were confronted by inflation, unemployment and declining production. In Romania, Slovakia, Bulgaria and the republics of the former Soviet Union, marketization was accompanied by substantial and growing hardship for many people. The extent of poverty in these countries might, it was feared, hinder the transition to a lasting system of democratic government.

Throughout the region, there was an explosion in the crime rate as a consequence of the flourishing black-market trade in abandoned military equipment, stolen cars and drugs. Much of the crime was organized by syndicates of gangsters and racketeers known collectively as the East European *mafia*. Occasionally, criminals even kidnapped western businessmen and

*With the end of the Cold War, many former military bases in Western Europe, like this one at Greenham Common in England, were abandoned as US force levels in Europe were reduced.*

tourists, holding them to ransom. Fear of crime proved sufficient by 1993 to slow the stream of western visitors to some parts of Eastern Europe.

At the same time, western politicians and diplomats were concerned by the growth of national intolerance and by the power that was still retained by persons closely connected to the former communist governments. The reappearance in a few countries of communist-style methods of rule, such as the use of secret police, censorship and harassment of political opponents, was equally alarming.

# ECONOMIC ASSISTANCE

Western governments were swift to grant economic assistance to Eastern Europe. It was in the interests of western governments to maintain stability in the region and to ensure a speedy transition to market economies. Large sums of emergency aid were given to the countries of Eastern Europe, such as the grant of over 100 million dollars to Czechoslovakia from the United States. Thereafter, assistance usually took the form of loans to businesses to help them become more efficient and purchase up-to-date machinery.

In 1991 the International Monetary Fund lent 5,000 million dollars to Eastern Europe on behalf of the most advanced western countries. The European Bank for Reconstruction and Development, which was set up in 1990 to invest in Eastern Europe, allocated 9,000 million dollars to the region between 1991 and 1994. The European Community and its member states gave over 10,000 million ecus in grants and loans to Eastern Europe in the period 1989-91.

Despite their size, these huge amounts proved insufficient for the needs of the East European countries. Much of the money had to be used by the East European governments simply to pay off debts they had already incurred in Western Europe and the United States.

Nevertheless, western countries were able to use their financial resources to put political pressure on the governments of the region. By linking assistance to political reform, they were able to speed up the move towards democracy and to reduce the threat of neo-communism. When, therefore, in June 1990 the Romanian president ordered his private army of miners to attack political protesters, western assistance to

Romania was immediately cut back. It was only restored after the president had promised to use more peaceful methods of persuasion in the future.

All the countries of Eastern Europe believed that their economies would greatly benefit from joining the European Community. By 1993, Hungary, Poland, Romania, the Czech Republic and Slovakia had been granted associate EC membership. In return, the governments of all five had to agree to respect human rights and not to return to communist-style methods of rule.

Many East Europeans grumbled that Western Europe had not given their countries sufficient assistance to help the move from communism to a market economy. Much of Western Europe, however, was in deep recession during the early 1990s and therefore lacked the wealth to give all the help which Eastern Europe needed. In addition, the example of East Germany, which experienced an upsurge in unemployment despite having received 60,000 million dollars worth of aid and loans from the former West Germany, suggested that pumping money into Eastern Europe was not the solution to every economic problem.

By coupling economic assistance to political reforms, Western Europe skilfully strengthened the new democratic order in Eastern Europe. However, when it came to dealing with nationalism and its consequences, western politicians proved less capable.

## WESTERN EUROPE AND YUGOSLAVIA

During the early 1990s, most Western European politicians seemed to believe that nationalism was no longer an important force in European affairs. Instead, they thought that there was a tendency among nations to want to co-operate, even to the extent of joining together in one state. At a meeting of European leaders at Maastricht in 1991, plans were drawn up to make the European Community into a single, unified super-state.

The eruption of national hatred in Yugoslavia came therefore as a surprise to most Western European politicians. At first they believed that the Serbian politicians were only bluffing and that they would never resort to force. Failing to take either Milosevic or the power of nationalism seriously, they

The continued inability of the European Community and most western powers individually to devise a credible strategy towards the Balkan war heralds an escalating diplomatic and foreign policy shambles. . . . The mixture of western inertia, misreading of Balkan politics and incompetence, has greatly reduced western standing. . . . Post-communist governments, whether in Budapest, Sofia or Warsaw, cannot afford to voice criticisms into the face of the EC or other western government representatives. In private, however, the West's utter failure to implement a workable foreign policy towards the Balkans has cast much doubt on the political future of the European Community.

From *East European Newsletter* (10 August 1992).

watched in bewilderment as war broke out and then spread in 1992 from Croatia to Bosnia-Herzegovina. Having first attempted in vain to negotiate a settlement through the European Community, western politicians were forced to hand the matter over to the United Nations. As it turned out, however, the United Nations itself lacked the manpower, resources and political will to impose peace and put a stop to the conflict.

Even with the fighting at its height, western politicians were convinced that the protagonists could be made to see sense and to reach an agreement. Most were unwilling to consider the view that the only way this could be achieved would be to send a large NATO intervention force to keep the warring sides apart.

The lesson of the civil war in Yugoslavia was that Western Europe was ready to give aid and loans to Eastern Europe but was not prepared to use military means to protect East Europeans from wars and violence of their own making. By not acting firmly to stop the fighting in the former Yugoslavia, western governments may, however, have actually increased the likelihood of war breaking out somewhere else in the region.

*The threat of full-scale war in the Russian Federation was brought one step closer when, in 1994, the government of the small Russian republic of Chechnya, which is mainly Muslim, declared its independence. Fighting broke out between the Russian army and troops loyal to the Chechen government at the end of the year. This picture show Chechen fighters in the capital Grozny, shooting at advancing Russian soldiers in the city centre.*

# CONCLUSION

The countries of Eastern Europe have always had much in common. For most of their history, these countries have been economically and socially backward and ruled as part of foreign empires. All suffered tremendous devastation and population loss during the Second World War and then, at the end of the war, had communism imposed upon them by the Soviet Union. After more than forty years, a combination of economic failure and changes in the Soviet leadership resulted in the collapse of communism throughout Eastern Europe.

During the 1990s, however, it became increasingly obvious that Eastern Europe could no longer be considered a single region but several. Although the transition to a market economy and to democracy proved harder than most people had imagined, the Czech Republic, Hungary and Poland gave every appearance of political stability and of rapid economic progress. All three countries may be expected to gain full membership of the European Community around the year 2000. The pace of political and economic reform was much slower, however, in Slovakia, Romania and Bulgaria and the future of these countries must be considered much more uncertain. Some specialists maintain that it may take them half a century to catch up economically with the countries of Western Europe.

In the Balkans and the former Soviet Union, the prospects for peace and economic progress remain particularly bleak. It is unlikely that an enduring settlement can be made in the former Yugoslavia without massive and sustained military intervention. It is equally improbable that the economy of Russia and of most of the countries of the former Soviet Union can be put on a secure footing without equally large western investment and aid. Since the military and financial resources of Western Europe and the United States are limited, the opportunities thrown up by the collapse of communism may be lost in a large part of Eastern Europe.

# GLOSSARY

**Balkans**
South-eastern Europe, including Romania, Bulgaria, Albania, Greece, and the former Yugoslavia.

**Capitalism**
System based upon a market economy and upon the private ownership of factories, farms and businesses.

**Censorship**
When the government regularly forbids the publication of information in newspapers and the media.

**Class enemy**
Usually a member of the middle or upper class who is considered to oppose the interests of the working class. Used by the communists as a term of abuse for all who disagreed with their ideas or methods.

**Cold War**
Situation which existed between 1945 and the late 1980s when relations between Western Europe and the United States on the one hand and Eastern Europe and the Soviet Union on the other were as bad as they could be without an actual 'hot' war breaking out.

**Collectives**
Large farms and businesses operated by the state.

**Coup d'état**
Sudden seizure of power in a country, often undertaken violently and with the help of the army.

**Democracy**
A state in which the government is chosen by the people in free, fair and frequent elections.

**Ethnic cleansing**
Forcible removal from an area of people belonging to a different nationality.

**Federal**
When a state is organized into republics each of which is allowed a measure of self-government.

**General strike**
When all the workers in a country, and not just in one industry, go on strike.

**Industrialization**
Development and growth of industry.

**Market economy**
Economy where producers fix their own production targets and prices and compete against each other to sell goods to the public. In a market economy, most businesses are privately owned.

**Marketization**
Move from a planned, state-owned economy to a market economy.

**Martial law**
When the armed services take over the police and courts in a country and judge offenders by military law. Military laws and penalties are usually more severe than the corresponding civilian ones.

**Multinational state**
A state in which two or more nations live.

**Nationality**
A population group usually sharing the same language and culture.

**Nationalism**
The belief that the world is organized into nations, that allegiance to one's nation should take first place above all other loyalties, and that the best form of state is the nation state.

**Nation state**
A state in which members of a single nation make up nearly all the state's population.

**Neo-communism**
When power and influence is held in a state by former members of the Communist Party, who often continue using typically communist methods of rule.

**Planned economy**
Economy in which factories, farms and businesses decide on production levels, targets and prices on the basis of a plan previously drawn up by managers and government officials.

**Political prisoner**
Person imprisoned for his or her political beliefs.

**Prague Spring**
Period from January to August 1968 when Czechoslovakia was ruled by the moderate communist, Alexander Dubcek. Prague was the capital city of Czechoslovakia.

**Privatize**
To convert state-owned industries into privately owned ones.

**Satellite-states**
States which closely follow policies laid down by another state.

**Solidarity**
Trade union established in Poland in 1980. In 1989, Solidarity became a political party and triumphed in the elections held in Poland that year.

# TIMELINE

**1878** — Bulgaria, Serbia and Romania declared independent states and no longer a part of the Turkish Empire.

**1914-18** — First World War.

**1917** — Russian Revolution followed by communist seizure of power.

**1919-20** — Boundaries of Eastern Europe redrawn at the Paris Peace Conference.

**1928** — Stalin becomes leader of Soviet Union.

**1939-45** — The Second World War.

**1945-48** — Communists seize power in Eastern Europe.

**1949** — Communist East German state established.

**1953** — Death of Stalin; Stalin is succeeeded as leader by Nikita Khrushchev.
Anti-communist rebellion in East Germany.

**1956** — Hungarian Revolution.

**1968** — Prague Spring and Soviet invasion of Czechoslovakia.

**1980** — Solidarity trade union founded in Poland.

**1981** — General Jaruzelski declares martial law.

**1985** — Mikhail Gorbachev becomes leader of Soviet Union.

**1989** — *June:* Free elections in Poland.
*August:* Solidarity government takes power in Poland.
*September:* Hungary allows East Germans to cross its border and travel to West Germany.
*October:* Hungary declares itself no longer a communist state.
Demonstrations in East German cities.
Fortieth anniversary celebrations of East Germany.
*November:* East German government collapses; the Berlin Wall is opened.
Demonstrations in Czechoslovakia; Czechoslovak communists resign from power.
Bulgarian communist leader arrested.
*December:* Bulgarian communists promise to hold free elections.
Romanian communist leader overthrown.
Vaclav Havel becomes president of Czechoslovakia.

**1990** — *March:* Elections held in East Germany and Hungary.
Fighting briefly erupts between Romanians and Hungarians in the Romanian city of Tirgu Mures.
*June:* Elections held in Bulgaria, Czechoslovakia and Romania.
Miners attack demonstrators in Bucharest.
*October:* Unification of Germany.

**1991** — *March:* New multi-party government set up in Albania.
*August:* Attempted *coup d'état* in Soviet Union; Communist Party banned.
*September:* Fighting breaks out between Serb and Croat forces in Croatia.
*October:* Union of Democratic Forces wins election in Bulgaria.
*December:* Soviet Union abolished.

**1992** — *April:* Fighting breaks out in Bosnia-Herzegovina between Serbs, Croats and Bosnian Muslims.
*October:* Ex-communist Democratic Labour Party wins election in Lithuania.
*December:* Czechoslovakia replaced by Czech Republic and Slovakia.

**1993** — *September:* Elections in Poland result in strong gains by the ex-commu nist Union of the Democratic Left.
*October:* President Yeltsin closes down Russian Congress of People's Deputies.
*December:* Elections for the new State Duma in Russia result in Vladimir Zhirinovsky's Liberal Democrats becoming the largest party.

**1994** — *May:* Hungarian Socialist Party wins election in Hungary.
*December*: Russian president Boris Yeltsin sends troops into the breakaway republic of Chechnya.

# FURTHER READING

**Almond, Mark** *A Paper House: The Ending of Yugoslavia* (Hutchinson Radius, 1992).

**Almond, Mark** *The Rise and Fall of Nicolae and Elena Ceausescu* (Chapmans, London, 1992).

**Batt, Judy** *East/Central Europe: From Reform to Transformation* (Royal Institute of International Affairs, 1991).

**Beloff, Nora** *Tito's Flawed Legacy* (Victor Gollancz, London, 1985).

**Brogan, Patrick** *Eastern Europe 1939-89: The Fifty Years War* (Bloomsbury, London, 1990).

**Davies, Norman** *God's Playground: A History of Poland*, Volume 2 (Oxford University Press, 1981).

**Dawisha, Karen** *Eastern Europe, Gorbachev and Reform: The Great Challenge* (Cambridge University Press, 1990).
*Eastern Europe and the Commonwealth of Independent States 1992* (Europa, London, 1992).

**Frankland, Mark** *The Patriots' Revolution: How Eastern Europe Won its Freedom* (Sinclair-Stevenson, London, 1990).

**Fulbrook, Mary** *The Two Germanies 1945-90* (Macmillan, London, 1992).

**Garton Ash, Timothy** *We the People: The Revolutions of '89 Witnessed in Warsaw, Budapest, Berlin and Prague* (Granta Books and Penguin, 1990).

**Gati, Charles** *The Bloc that Failed: Soviet/East European Relations in Transition* (Indiana University Press, Bloomington and Indianapolis, 1990).

**Glenny, Misha** *The Fall of Yugoslavia: The Third Balkan War* (Penguin Books, 1992).
*The Rebirth of History: Eastern Europe in the Age of Democracy* (Penguin Books, 1990).

**Harbor, Bernard** *Conflict in Eastern Europe* (Wayland, Hove, 1993)

**Hoensch, Jorg** *A History of Modern Hungary 1867-1986* (Longman, 1988).

**Hosking, Geoffrey** *A History of the Soviet Union* (Fontana, 1990).

**Jones, Derek (ed)** *And the Walls Came Tumbling Down: Eastern Europe after the Revolutions* (Channel 4, 1990).

**Okey, Robin** *Eastern Europe 1740-1985: Feudalism to Communism* (Unwin Hyman, London, 1985).

**Rady, Martyn** *Romania in Turmoil: A Contemporary History* (I.B. Tauris, London, 1992).
*The Breakup of Yugoslavia* (Wayland, Hove, 1994).

**Rupnik, Jacques** *The Other Europe* (Weidenfeld and Nicolson, London 1988).

**Shawcross, William** *Dubcek and Czechoslovakia 1918-1990* (Hogarth Press, London, 1990).

**Singleton, Fred** *A Short History of the Yugoslav Peoples* (Cambridge University Press, 1985).

**Stokes, Gale** *From Stalinism to Pluralism: A Documentary History of Eastern Europe since 1945* (Oxford University Press, 1991).

**Ramet, Sabrina** *Social Currents in Eastern Europe* (Duke University Press, Durham and London, 1991).

**Sword, Keith** *The Times Guide to Eastern Europe* (Times Books, 1991)

**The Observer** *Tearing Down the Curtain: The People's Revolution in Eastern Europe* (Hodder and Stoughton, London, 1990).

**Toranska, Teresa** *Oni: Stalin's Polish Puppets* (Collins Harvill, London, 1987).

# INDEX